NO HEELS, NO PROBLEM

of related interest

Stumbling Through Space and Time
Living Life with Dyspraxia
Rosemary Richings
ISBN 978 1 83997 269 0
eISBN 978 1 83997 270 6

ADHD Girls to Women
Getting on the Radar
Lotta Borg Skoglund
Foreword by Professor Susan Young
ISBN 978 1 80501 054 8
eISBN 978 1 80501 055 5
AUDIOBOOK ISBN 978 1 39981 238 2

Young, Autistic and ADHD
Moving into adulthood when you're multiply-neurodivergent
Sarah Boon
ISBN 978 1 83997 673 5
eISBN 978 1 83997 674 2
AUDIOBOOK ISBN 978 1 39982 087 5

ADHD an A–Z
Figuring it Out Step by Step
Leanne Maskell
ISBN 978 1 83997 385 7
eISBN 978 1 83997 386 4
AUDIOBOOK ISBN 978 1 39980 421 9

No Heels, No Problem

A Neurodivergent Survival Guide to Adult Life when you are Dyspraxic or ADHD

MAXINE ROPER

Foreword by Rosemary Richings

Jessica Kingsley Publishers
London and Philadelphia

First published in Great Britain in 2025 by Jessica Kingsley Publishers
An imprint of John Murray Press

1

Copyright © Maxine Roper 2025

The right of Maxine Roper to be identified as the Author of the Work has been asserted by her in accordance with the Copyright, Designs and Patents Act 1988.

Foreword copyright © Rosemary Richings 2025

Front cover image source: Nicola Powling.

All rights reserved. No part of this publication may be reproduced, stored in a retrieval system, or transmitted, in any form or by any means without the prior written permission of the publisher, nor be otherwise circulated in any form of binding or cover other than that in which it is published and without a similar condition being imposed on the subsequent purchaser.

Content Warning: This book mentions alcoholism, suicide and mental health.

The information contained in this book is not intended to replace the services of trained medical professionals or to be a substitute for medical advice. You are advised to consult a doctor on any matters relating to your health, and in particular on any matters that may require diagnosis or medical attention.

A CIP catalogue record for this title is available from the British Library and the Library of Congress

ISBN 978 1 83997 228 7
eISBN 978 1 83997 229 4

Printed and bound in Great Birtain by Clays Ltd.

Jessica Kingsley Publishers' policy is to use papers that are natural, renewable and recyclable products and made from wood grown in sustainable forests. The logging and manufacturing processes are expected to conform to the environmental regulations of the country of origin.

Jessica Kingsley Publishers
Carmelite House
50 Victoria Embankment
London EC4Y 0DZ

www.jkp.com

John Murray Press
Part of Hodder & Stoughton Ltd
An Hachette Company

The authorised representative in the EEA is Hachette Ireland,
8 Castlecourt Centre, Dublin 15, D15 XTP3, Ireland (email: info@hbgi.ie)

Contents

First Page Note — 9
Foreword by Rosemary Richings — 10

Introduction — 12
- About this book — 13
- What you'll find in this book — 14
- What you won't find in this book — 17
- About me and why I wrote this book — 21

1: Finding Out About Dyspraxia and ADHD — 27
Or 'I Think This is Me!' What Exactly are Dyspraxia and ADHD – and What *aren't* They?
- Dyspraxia — 28
- ADHD — 32
- Misconceptions about neurodivergence more generally — 40
- Dyspraxia and ADHD: The dream team — 41
- What causes dyspraxia and ADHD (and what doesn't) — 42
- Final thoughts — 43

2: Self-Understanding — **45**
'So, THAT'S Why I Feel This Way...?'

- Some feelings and experiences you might relate to if you're neurodivergent — 45
- 'Is this REALLY me...?' Dealing with doubt — 55
- 'Is this a neurodivergent thing or just a "me" thing?' — 56
- Final thoughts — 57

3: Should I Get Assessed Professionally? — **58**

- 'Do I need a professional diagnosis?' — 59
- Myths about diagnosis — 65
- 'Where do I go for a professional diagnosis?' — 67
- Things to know about assessments — 72
- Other ways to get the most from your assessment — 75
- 'What if I don't get a diagnosis?' — 77
- 'What about self-diagnosis?' (Spoiler: Yes, it's absolutely fine) — 79
- 'Why is there so much confusion between different types of neurodivergence? How do I know which I am?' — 81
- Final thoughts — 82

4: 'So This is Me! What Now?' — **84**
'Coming Out' as Neurodivergent

- 'Is it normal to feel this way?' Feeling your feelings about being neurodivergent — 85
- 'So what do I do now?' — 87
- Talking to people in your life about neurodivergence — 89
- 'Should I tell someone else if I think they're neurodivergent?' — 94
- 'Should I tell others about someone else's neurodivergence?' — 96
- 'Should I tell my employer, or potential employers, about my neurodivergence?' — 99
- Final thoughts — 102

5: Other People's Reactions — **104**
The Best, the Worst and How to Handle Them

- The best reactions you can hope for — 105
- Other common reactions — 105
- And common questions — 106
- The worst reactions — 107
- Well-meant but tricky compliments — 110
- If you struggle to react to questions... — 110

- If it's difficult to tell how the conversation is going... 111
- If someone you really care about reacts badly... 112
- If you feel someone's reaction discriminates against you... 115
- Dealing with past relationships 119
- Final thoughts 123

6: Sharing Your Story with the World 125
- Ways to share your experiences 126
- Privacy issues around story sharing 137
- Final thoughts 138

7: Being Kind to Your Mind 139
Or 'This Can't be "Growing Pains" Anymore!'
- Recognizing your inner critic 140
- Finding support for your neurodivergence 149
- Final thoughts 159

8: How Medication Works for Me 161
- How medication works and can help 162
- Medication mythbusters 165
- Tips for your first week of stimulants and beyond 169
- Final thoughts 173

9: Looking After Your Body 175
Or 'Why Didn't They Tell Us This at School?!'
- Neurodivergence and food (or 'Why it's easier for me to make you a wedding cake than a sandwich') 176
- Dyspraxic dreads: Eating, drinking and cooking in groups 179
- Neurodivergence, drink and drugs 181
- Neurodivergence and sleep 183
- Neurodivergence and exercise (or 'Yes, I found some I actually enjoyed...') 186
- Neurodivergence and your cycle (hormones, not bikes...) 188
- Smear tests 190
- How to look good as a neurodivergent person (You don't need heels...) 192
- Neurodivergent body behaviours that don't go in cute memes... 196
- Neurodivergence and weather 199
- Final thoughts 201

10: Getting Around and Driving — **202**
Or 'How Do I Make Getting Around Easier? Will I Ever Learn to Drive?'
- Life without driving — 203
- A neurodivergent's guide to driving: My long and winding road to passing a driving test — 209
- Final thoughts — 224

11: Making Sense of Relationships — **226**
Or 'Why is There So Much Drama in My Life?'
- Ways neurodivergence can explain your relationships — 228
- Neurodivergence and your sex life (or 'Sex talk that doesn't sound as if it's from your embarrassed aunty'...) — 234
- The tough stuff in relationships: From conflict to grief — 239
- Final (nice) thought — 243

12: Ten Things I Wish I'd Known in My Twenties — **245**
Or 'The Whole Book, Summed Up'
- Finally... — 250

Further Reading — 251
- Dyspraxia — 251
- ADHD — 252
- Autism — 253
- Dyscalculia — 253
- Dyslexia — 254
- Being multiply neurodivergent — 254

Further Information and Support — 255
- Need help right now? — 255
- Types of neurodivergence — 256
- Support for all neurodivergences — 257
- Other support (A–Z) — 257

References and Bibliography — 261
Acknowledgements — 264
Index — 266

First Page Note

If you find books hard to start or finish
It's common for adults with ADHD and other neurodivergent identities to feel overwhelmed by reading or struggle to sit down with a book because of attention difficulties, reading difficulties, or both. If you loved books at school and now have to fight your way through an unread pile to get to your bed, or there's a row of unfinished e-books on your reading device, that's also common. To address this, this book has been organized so it's as easy as possible to follow and to dip in and out of. To help you, there are recaps at the end of each chapter...

A quick content note
This book mentions some heavy topics, including discrimination, mental health, addiction, bereavement and suicide. While I've made every effort not to cause distress, do take care if these topics are challenging for you. There are details of organizations offering information and support at the end of the book.

Foreword

Rosemary Richings

I have dedicated much of my writing career to educating people about neurodivergence. I also wrote *Stumbling Through Space and Time: Living Life with Dyspraxia* (2022). Through my work, I have learned that the neurodivergent lived experience literary market is steadily growing. Yet these stories aren't as widely shared, distributed and read as they should be.

Many books by neurodivergent authors don't get the same level of publicity as airport-friendly fiction. Fortunately, this reality might change over time. That necessary change seemed possible when the BBC greenlit Elle McNicoll's *A Kind of Spark*. The show did exceptionally well on streaming platforms. That's far better than the representation and research available when I was first diagnosed.

When I was a little girl, I was diagnosed with dyspraxia. All my family got was an outdated pamphlet about clumsy child syndrome. As an adult woman who's still as dyspraxic as ever, my entire existence is proof of how wrong that pamphlet is. I was also once told something just as incorrect: dyspraxic women are a medical rarity. Women are under-researched in studies about neurological conditions, complicating the process of having our support needs taken seriously.

As a result, being neurodivergent and a woman is a guessing game. Those with the power to provide support often make assumptions about what we need. We all experience neurodivergence differently, meaning there's always more to learn about how our brains work. Lived-experience perspectives make that continuous learning process possible. When I read *No Heels, No Problem*, I was presented with a book that delivers on that promise and much more.

One notable example was Maxine's story of dealing with the judgement of others for not successfully acquiring a driver's licence the moment she was old enough. She told readers why and how she got a driver's licence in adulthood, not her teenage years. After all, isn't the important part that she made it happen because she felt it was essential to learn, not how old she was when it happened?

Without having a neurodivergent peer to talk to, reaching independence milestones, such as driving, slower than peers may be internalized as something to be ashamed of. She answers many of the questions you likely have about being a neurodivergent woman, plus several questions you were likely too embarrassed to ask. *No Heels, No Problem* is a therapeutic mechanism that helps you let go of any feelings of shame that may be preventing you from living life on your terms.

Introduction

- Are you a dyspraxic or ADHD woman, or do you think you might be?
- Does a lot of life advice for women feel as if it's not quite meant for you?
- Does your life always seem to bounce between highs and lows?
- Were you told you'd grow out of dyspraxia or ADHD as a child, not grow into them as a woman?

If you want to understand what dyspraxia and ADHD mean to you as an adult, and a woman, this book is for you.

For any young woman, the world can be brilliant and overwhelming. For dyspraxic and ADHD women, the freedom and choices that go with being an adult can feel even more brilliant and overwhelming. In many ways, getting to your twenties might seem like a relief, and an exciting chance for you to live the life you want to. But the jump from having your days planned out for you at school (whether you like it or not), to being in charge of yourself (and maybe other people), probably also hasn't been that easy for you.

There are times when growing up feels less like having the freedom to do what you love and more like being handed a set of car keys and told to drive to the other end of the country when you've never driven (and driving might be a sore subject for you too...). You might have had support at school if your dyspraxia and/or ADHD were recognized when you were younger. But the wobble board exercises you did when you were seven, or the extra geometry practice you had at lunchtime, probably don't seem to have much to do with your life as a grown-up. If the knowledge came later or is new to you, heading out into the world has probably given you a lot of questions that have led to where you are now.

About this book

No Heels, No Problem is a straight-talking survival guide for young dyspraxic and ADHD women, written by me, an adult-diagnosed dyspraxic and ADHD woman who made it through her twenties without owning a pair of high heels. Understanding your neurodivergent self deserves more than an inspirational hashtag, or the same few dreary study and work tips you've read before. This book will support you in every part of your neurodiversity journey, from discovery and diagnosis to everything beyond. Based on everything I've learned from my twenties, it'll help you understand what dyspraxia and ADHD mean to you as a woman, in your relationship with others, yourself and your body. As well as uplifting humour, there are honest neurodivergent takes on life's rock bottoms like anxiety, depression, grief and loss. Think of it as an all-you-can-eat buffet of experience and advice, with no chance of spilling food down yourself. Or a coffee with someone who's seen the best and worst of life and is ready to cheer you on when you're doing great and be there for you when you fall. (Metaphorically or literally...)

What you'll find in this book

This book is about being dyspraxic and having ADHD because I have both those diagnoses. Other types of neurodivergence and certain other health conditions can look like or commonly go with either of them. These are listed at the end of the book, alongside links to further reading and support.

As I've mentioned already, all the information here has been organized in the most ADHD-friendly way possible. Each chapter is a mixture of tip lists and answers to important questions. There are also handy boxes throughout the book to help you remember what you've read, and tell you where you can find more information on certain topics.

Chapter 1 has everything you need to know if you're new to neurodivergence; starting with what dyspraxia and ADHD are and how they go together.

Chapter 2 is about feelings and experiences that often go along with neurodivergence, especially for women who've grown up without recognition or the right support. If you were diagnosed as a child rather than recently, it can also help you start to understand who you are as a grown-up.

Chapter 3 is a rough practical guide to how getting a professional diagnosis of dyspraxia and/or ADHD works in the UK, including when you need one and when you don't, and why self-diagnosis is valid.

Chapter 4 is a guide to how you might be feeling after a diagnosis, whether it's recent or whether you've just started learning about an early diagnosis as an adult. It also looks at how you might be feeling about past relationships after learning more about yourself.

Chapter 5 is about how people in your life might react to your diagnosis, from the best to the worst reactions, and everything in between.

Chapter 6 is a guide to sharing your experiences of neurodivergence in public if you want to, whether it's through creating online content or appearing in the media.

Unrecognized neurodivergent women can spend years believing the very worst things about themselves. In **Chapter 7**, I'll tell you from my own experience how to replace some of those horrible old insults in your head with new and nicer ways of understanding who you are. From counselling and coaching to medication for ADHD, you'll also find out more about what support there is for neurodivergence and how to get the best from it – especially on a tight budget.

If you're an adult who's considering starting medication for ADHD, **Chapter 8** busts some common myths and has some tips for the first few weeks from my own experience.

Chapter 9 is about looking after your body. Being neurodivergent with a woman's body can be tough in ways you probably didn't learn about at school and which aren't talked about much in the mainstream media, or aren't recognized as being part of neurodivergence. From hunting for smart shoes you won't fall over in, to the monthly mess of periods, this chapter is a frank head-to-toe guide to them all.

Chapter 10 is about getting around and driving. Being neurodivergent can make it harder to learn to drive. If you're a learner, a new driver, a non-driver or undecided about whether to learn, this chapter has something for you. There's advice on finding an instructor who understands your brain, the things 'they' don't tell you to expect after you pass your test, as well as life without driving, and dealing with people who are strangely bothered about why you 'still' don't have your licence.

Chapter 11 is all about you and the people in your life. Being neurodivergent can be part of the reason why you have brilliant people around you. It can also make you more likely to get into situations with other people which aren't so helpful. This chapter is about the drama dyspraxia and ADHD can add to all kinds of relationships.

Finally, in **Chapter 12**, I'll bring together what's in the book and tell you the ten things I wish I'd known about life in my twenties.

At the end of the book there are two sections, one with links to further reading and one with links to support organizations.

What I've written largely comes from my lived experience because it's what I'm best qualified to write about. I hope you feel it speaks to you, but if you feel it doesn't, the best advice I can give you is to write or talk about yours in any way that helps you.

What you won't find in this book

- **Advice about children or parenting:** There are numerous other books for teachers and parents on how to support neurodivergent children. Teachers and parents who are neurodivergent themselves can often offer you great advice.

- **Career advice:** There is no one job that's better or worse if you're neurodivergent and no advice that works for any job. Although I have written and spoken elsewhere about some of my experiences in the workplace, I've chosen not to in this book for a number of reasons. If you're looking for detailed information on getting support for neurodivergence at work, or supporting neurodivergent people at work, my good friend Alice Hewson (2024) has written an excellent book, *Neurodiversity in the Workplace: How to Create an Inclusive and Safe Environment*.

- **Loads of productivity tips:** There are plenty of these online, and three of the most popular ADHD content creators have written books of them. See: *How to ADHD* by Jess McCabe (2024), Dani Donovan's (2022) *The Anti-Planner* and Meredith Carder's (2024) *It All Makes Sense Now*.

- **Loads of absolute statements:** 'Neurodivergence makes you a people pleaser.' 'Neurodivergence makes you cheat on your partner/commit crime.' I'll explain why not in the next chapter...

'Help! I'm worried that I/my daughter will never be able to work, get married or have children!'

Can a woman do all those things with dyspraxia and ADHD? Yes! And some have done them all without any diagnosis or support. Should you want all those things for your daughter/sister/friend? Yes, if she wants them for herself. But having none of those things doesn't make you less of an adult or less of a person. This is a support book, not an instruction manual. I can't promise you any particular life, and nor should any book or any person. I do want to promise that by the end of this book, you'll understand yourself better and like yourself more, whatever life you're living.

Words I use in this book (and some I don't)

Neurodiversity is the idea that people think and learn differently. Credited to Australian sociologist Judy Singer, it was first widely used in the autism community in the 1990s. It's now used in relation to a group of neurological conditions, which includes autism, ADHD, dyspraxia, dyslexia, dyscalculia and Tourette's syndrome. These conditions share similarities and differences, and two or more of them often go together in one person, but not always, or to the same extent. It can also be said to include a wider range of neurological and mental health conditions, which not everyone agrees with.

Neurodivergent is often used as an umbrella term for the neurological conditions named above, or a person with one or more of these conditions. It's a socio-political not a medical term, like 'ethnic minority' or 'LGBTQIA+' (lesbian, gay, bisexual, transgender, queer, intersex, asexual). I use it for convenience when I'm referring to multiple conditions under the umbrella, to people who are exploring their diagnosis, or people who, like me, have more than one diagnosis. It's not meant to replace condition labels where they're needed and helpful. It shouldn't be used as either a compliment, euphemism or insult. Although it was first used by autistic people, it isn't another word for 'autistic', and you should refer to autism specifically if that's what you mean.

Neurotypical means someone whose abilities are within a similar range and who thinks and learns in a way which is seen as common or 'the norm', a bit like 'straight' or 'able-bodied'. It's not a slur or insult, although some might use it when they're annoyed or frustrated.

Wherever possible, I use **I/we/you** when talking about dyspraxia and ADHD, not 'they' or 'people with', because I'm writing about something I live with, and this book is for you, not about you.

The medical and professional term for **dyspraxia** is developmental coordination disorder or DCD. I'm using dyspraxia even though it's an outdated term, as it's still more widely used and understood in the UK where I'm from.

Most people prefer **identity-first** rather than person-first language: as in 'I'm dyspraxic' or 'Maxine is dyspraxic', not 'I have dyspraxia' or 'Maxine has dyspraxia'. This reflects the idea that these labels are something part of you rather than something wrong with you. Identity-first language is more difficult with ADHD because you can't say 'I'm ADHD', so I tend to say 'I have ADHD', but I also tend to say 'ADHDers', 'the ADHD community' or 'ADHD people' rather than 'people with ADHD'.

I don't describe myself or anyone else as 'suffering' from dyspraxia or ADHD, any more than I would say I 'suffer from' being a woman, or my friends 'suffer from' the colour of their skin. We may suffer or be disadvantaged because of those things, but using that word reduces us to our suffering. I personally don't mind the phrase 'living with dyspraxia/ADHD' as much, but I know many others don't like it.

I don't use functioning labels for ADHD and autism (like 'mild/severe' and 'high/low functioning') and these are now widely discouraged as they can be misleading. Labels like 'mild' or 'high-functioning' often mean people aren't recognized as needing support, while 'severe' or 'low functioning' can be demeaning to people and may underestimate their ability or quality of life. If you're talking about someone's needs, it's best to be factual and specific. For example: 'Joy sees a support worker once a week to help her with XYZ related to her ADHD' or 'Jamie is autistic with learning disabilities and lives in residential care'.

ADD, Asperger's syndrome, PDD and NLD are outdated and/or rarely used labels. Some people, especially older adults, may still use and/or identify with them. Most people prefer to identify as ADHD, autistic, dyspraxic or multiply neurodivergent.

Everyone has different relationships with words. If you're interacting with or referring to someone directly, it's always best to ask them what they prefer.

INTRODUCTION

About me and why I wrote this book

Like most neurodivergent women my age, I was diagnosed as an adult rather than in childhood. I was born prematurely, which is now understood to be linked to neurodivergence but back then just meant I was the subject of playground gossip and medical misinformation that kids had picked up from home. I grew from a critically ill baby into a girl who never caught a cold and was always reading or writing stories. As a child and teenager in the 90s, I had an inkling that I was different but never quite knew why. As the inkling grew, I increasingly turned to self-help books and personality quizzes. They often suggested that to enjoy life, you needed a certain kind of personality; usually the kind I'd been told I didn't have. The more progressive ones assured me that it was okay to be different and to be myself. But they didn't really help me understand what my difference was and why 'being myself' felt problematic – let alone why I consistently got top grades in essay subjects and bottom grades in maths and science. Or why, at 17, I could design a website and interview someone as a journalist but not read a map, learn to drive, cook a meal or even make a presentable-looking sandwich.

Self-improvement was a big thing on TV then. There was a makeover show called *What Not to Wear*, which your friends and colleagues could nominate you for, and a dating show called *Would Like to Meet*, where three experts would send someone who'd been single for years out on a date, then watch it back and tell them everything they'd done wrong. If my memory serves me, there was the student who talked about her PhD ('too serious'), the man who was confused about how to order food (weird), the musician who chose a Polish restaurant for her first date ('not sexy' apparently, although you'd think millions of people in Poland somehow manage to enjoy both Polish food and sex...). But my favourite was a series called *Faking It*, where people would spend a month being taught how to do an unfamiliar job they seemed totally unsuited to, then take part in a skills contest along with three experienced pros, and a panel of expert judges had to spot the faker. Most participants seemed like me, anxious self-doubters who'd never left their home town, and they were transformed into confident go-getters. The message I took from this was that the only way to live was to pretend to be good at something I wasn't and turn into somebody I wasn't.

At 18, my desperation to become an adult yet inability to master most things that were expected of adults led to a breakdown. I made it to university after a 'gap year' which I largely spent unemployed and crying, but got there eventually, and it was then that my long journey to better understanding myself began. In the second year of my social sciences degree, a statistics module sneaked its way into my course. I went to see my tutor, who, unlike any of my teachers, recognized there might be a problem and cared enough to do something about it. She suggested I visit the university's service for students with disabilities. They referred me to an educational psychologist, who diagnosed me with dyspraxia.

In some ways, adult life was easier than life had ever felt before. I didn't have to do geometry, play netball or share a classroom with girls who made fun of my clothes. Having survived a breakdown and a statistics module, I graduated with the new Greek word for my brain and trained as a print journalist. Occasionally I saw my name in print, learned to love the dancefloor, and did unprintable things after free drinks in very nice surroundings. But in plenty of other ways, my twenties were harder than I'd ever imagined. I graduated a couple of years before the financial crash and landed a decently paid job, but lost that job because of my neurodivergence.

On top of trying to build a career with a badly understood

brain, I went through traumatic bereavement twice in three years. My uneven abilities due to my being neurodivergent created enough highs and lows to fill a screenplay. Women writers my age wrote about their lives in confessional memoirs, often touching on subjects like mental health, bad jobs, dating and friendships. Although I could relate to these women in many ways, I also knew that I experienced the world in some ways they didn't. Most of them talked about waiting tables or pulling pints to make ends meet. I was about as likely to win *The X Factor* as hold down a job in a bar. In fact, most people would probably prefer me to sing Madonna songs to them than pour them a beer while rushed off my feet. Women's magazines assumed I spent my life lusting after pretty shoes, which I mostly ignored because I couldn't walk in them.

Whenever I went looking for information about dyspraxia, there were just a few ancient websites, mostly for parents of dyspraxic children. The brilliant *Caged in Chaos*, a handbook for dyspraxic teenagers written by Vicky Biggs (first published in 2005, 2014) after she was diagnosed at 15, came out just before my diagnosis. But I was in my twenties, and the few other openly dyspraxic adults were decades older. The one book for adult dyspraxics that seemed to exist had a fusty section on sex and relationships which was more of a passion killer than the anti-depressants I took to write my dissertation. I'd known every study skills tip that actually helped me study since I was 15, and all the advice about the workplace was for jobs I'd never have.

Like many disabilities, dyspraxia seemed to be portrayed as something either superhuman or tragic. Dyspraxia either never held you back and gave you special powers that made you an asset to a City law firm; or meant you'd never amounted to anything. Very little of what I read spoke to me as a woman with a personality or a sense of humour. Feeling that dyspraxia deserved louder and better recognition, I became one of the first twentysomething women to write and speak about it in public. I wrote two articles for *The Guardian* and one for the *Daily Telegraph* where I interviewed dyspraxics about learning to drive. I spoke at events in every corner of the UK, from rural community centres to the House of Lords.

Although I'd been told dyspraxia was the reason for every difficulty I'd ever had, it didn't quite seem to explain everything. My reading habit had dwindled since leaving school, and despite being a professional writer, I rarely got through more than two books in a year. I couldn't sit down for more than a few minutes at a time when on my own, which, for a self-employed person mainly working alone, is not *exactly* ideal. In my thirties, a vibrant community of neurodivergent women started to emerge on social media. Like me, many were writers or working in creative industries. Most were autistic or ADHD women rather than dyspraxic, but many of their experiences looked like mine. Thanks to researchers like Professor Amanda Kirby, queen of the neurodiversity infographic, the world was starting to understand that conditions in the neurodiversity family often went together. At 36, in the middle of a pandemic, I was diagnosed with inattentive type ADHD, and given medication which helped me manage my attention and my life.

In all the years I spent trying to make sense of my brain, I was always looking for someone to be my cheerleader. Not a teenager waving pom-poms and doing the splits behind me while I wrote, which would be very annoying. But a reassuring older woman who'd been exactly where I was, knew exactly how I felt, and wanted the best for me. By the time my brain made sense to me, I was old enough to be that person myself. Now, I'm writing this book for women because it is the one I wish I'd had when I was younger.

In case you're wondering...

I will say a lot more about what dyspraxia and ADHD are and aren't in the next chapters. But I want to answer these two common questions first of all:

'How can you write a book if you have ADHD?'

This is the first book I've ever finished, at the age of 40, despite it being my life's ambition to write books for pretty much as long as I can remember. There's barely a time in my life when I haven't been trying to write one. 'Trying' being the operative word. Some years ago, someone on a shared computer accidentally opened a document containing an unfinished piece of my writing and asked with some concern if I'd been drunk while I wrote it. I assured them I hadn't, but when I looked at the document, I could see why they'd thought so. There were uncontrollably long sections, followed by paragraphs that were just one sentence or that trailed off in the middle. Although I've made a career out of writing, first as a journalist and now a content writer, probably the majority of things I've written have never been seen by anyone because they've never made it past this unfinished stage.

I now know that this is because I have ADHD and I am now able to write a book for two reasons: I have medication that helps me with focus, *and* two brilliant editors who've helped me organize my thoughts.

'How can you type if you're dyspraxic?'

Although home computers and mobile phones weren't widely used then, I taught myself to type from the age of six, probably because I hated writing by hand. As most dyspraxics now use computers and mobile phones pretty much from birth, most of us can type, but some of us may prefer audio typing or need extra support. Ask if you're not sure.

There are lots of other ADHD and/or dyspraxic women who write. I'll mention some in a moment, and there's a list of further reading at the end of the book.

CHAPTER 1

Finding Out About Dyspraxia and ADHD

Or 'I Think This is Me!' What Exactly are Dyspraxia and ADHD – and What *aren't* They?

As a woman reading this book, you're somewhere on the way to knowing something important about yourself that too many young women have lived too much of their lives not knowing about themselves. Dyspraxia, ADHD and autism in women were almost unrecognized and unheard of as recently as the last century. Over the time I've been writing this book, there's been an explosion of books and TV shows by neurodivergent women drawing on their experiences. Holly Smale, author of the book and Netflix series *Geek Girl* (2023), is dyspraxic and autistic, as is Elle McNicoll, author of the children's novel and TV series *A Kind of Spark* (2020). The Scottish sitcom *Dinosaur* is about the dating adventures of two sisters in their twenties: Nina, who is autistic and played by autistic actor Ashley Storrie, and Evie, whose ADHD is heavily implied. Meanwhile, comedian Shappi Khorsandi's (2023) memoir *Scatter Brain* and journalist Emma Mahony's (2021) *Better Late Than Never* are about recognizing their ADHD in midlife after decades of unexplained intensity and chaos.

Although all this recent visibility will I hope lead to change, it's thought that as many as three-quarters of neurodivergent women still don't know they are. Most diagnosed women have traits of more than one type of neurodivergence, but only one diagnosis. ADHD and dyspraxia often go together but one or both are missed. Dyspraxia is less likely to be recognized at all, and is often treated like a distant cousin of the other types of neurodivergence, being invited to the neurodiversity family party because someone's mum reminded everyone.

Dyspraxia and ADHD are possibly two of the most awkwardly and confusingly named conditions in the history of medicine. If I could, I'd happily give them both better names which would actually help people understand what they are. Some people prefer a 'strengths first' definition to the usual miserable lists of symptoms:

- Being really funny (but also clumsy, and lost without Google Maps).
- Having stacks of great ideas (but finding it hard to organize them so that they happen or arrive in your inbox when you want them).
- Being absolutely unbeatable at Scrabble (but having to bribe colleagues with biscuits for help with spreadsheets).

I prefer to start with a simple, neutral definition which isn't too perky or too gloomy.

Dyspraxia

Dyspraxia, officially known as developmental coordination disorder or DCD, means you have difficulty with coordination, movement and often spatial awareness. At school, you may have struggled with physical education (PE) and with anything practical, and with performing in front of people. You may also have found non-verbal reasoning subjects like maths and science hard, although not all dyspraxics do and this can also depend on how well you were taught. For adults, dyspraxia can make it harder to do things around the house, like cooking a meal from scratch, learning to drive, or working in retail jobs where speed and presentation are important. Most dyspraxic adults can do some hands-on tasks which are part of their daily routine, but it may take more effort, and new skills will always take a bit longer to learn. Dyspraxics may lose a lot of time to spilling things.

Dyspraxia as an official medical term has been out of use for decades. But most non-medics still use the old term rather than the medical name, probably because developmental coordination disorder is too long for the internet, and DCD sounds like something you spray on a frosty windscreen. There's no medical treatment for dyspraxic adults, as dyspraxia looks different in different people. But knowing you're dyspraxic will almost certainly make your life easier than not knowing. Things that are helpful or fun for people with better known types of neurodivergence may not be for dyspraxics. There are examples throughout the book.

Why *is* dyspraxia so ignored?

There are two possible reasons why I think dyspraxia is under-recognized. First, the sorts of hands-on tasks that dyspraxics tend to find hardest are often seen as easy and linked to jobs with low status. This makes people more likely to assume that someone who finds something difficult is either useless or thinks it's beneath them, rather than recognize that they're struggling and help them. People who make decisions in our society also tend to be those who don't have to do as many hands-on tasks or work in manual jobs themselves, so they might not appreciate how being dyspraxic could make life difficult. This was reflected in my family when I was growing up. My mum, who came from an east German family of labourers and trained as a carpenter, worried more about my lack of dexterity than my dad, whose family all did desk jobs and could afford to pay others to mend and do things.

A more positive reason dyspraxia gets less recognition than other types of neurodivergence might be that new tech and gadgets are making life much easier for dyspraxics all the time. In my lifetime, technology has widely replaced the need to wash dishes, handle loads of shopping bags or books, write by hand, draw diagrams, read maps and timetables or travel a long way for meetings. In another 50 or 100 years, self-driving cars might even mean nobody has to learn to drive.

That *doesn't* mean dyspraxia doesn't matter or won't matter in future. There will always be tasks that can't be done well enough by algorithms or machines. As I'll show throughout this book, there are times too when apps we rely on don't work. And not *all* technology is life-improving for us. It's taken ten years for me to manage self-service checkouts well enough that using one is actually quicker and won't end in me swearing while an electronic voice burbles: 'Unexpected item in bagging area…'

What dyspraxia is NOT

It can sometimes seem like there are more posts in the dyspraxic community asking whether dyspraxia is related to something else than there are about dyspraxia. Because it struggles to be recognized in its own right, there's a lot of confusion and misleading information out there about what dyspraxia is and isn't…

Dyspraxia is NOT dyslexia

If there were more dyspraxic graphic designers, we'd probably put this on a t-shirt. Dyspraxia and dyslexia are two similar-sounding Greek words for two different neurodivergent diagnoses.

Dyslexia is primarily a difficulty with reading and spelling, which dyspraxia is not. They sometimes go together, which can make recognizing them both harder. But on their own, they can look completely the opposite. Dyslexics can have nimble fingers and brilliant spatial awareness, while dyspraxics can be brilliant at reading and spelling. Some dyspraxics are even *hyperlexic* and could read fluently before they started school. Where dyspraxia and dyslexia *are* similar is the way they can make people feel about themselves without the right support.

Dyspraxia is NOT 'a mild form' of autism, ADHD or anything else

The reason for this misconception is because autism used to be diagnosed with functioning labels like mild-severe, or as sub-types with different names depending on their presentation, like Asperger's syndrome and nonverbal learning disorder. I explained back in the Introduction why functioning labels are often unhelpful and outdated, so head back there if you missed it. Describing dyspraxia as 'mild' autism or ADHD is even more unhelpful as it minimizes them all. You can be dyspraxic and autistic or ADHD. You can be one with significant traits of another. You can be one and little or nothing of the others. You can have traits of all three, or have all three professionally diagnosed if you want to and are able to. Some older adults may still identify with labels they were given as children, such as Asperger's syndrome or nonverbal learning disorder. However, people with these presentations are now diagnosed as autistic. There's no such thing as 'autism or ADHD lite', and thinking of dyspraxia that way is not good for anyone.

> There's more about getting assessed professionally in the next chapter. Read on for more about ADHD.

ADHD

ADHD stands for attention deficit hyperactivity disorder, although this doesn't really describe it at all. A 'deficit' means lack of attention. What ADHDers *actually* have is difficulty managing or regulating attention to things, which means paying the right amount of attention to the right thing at the right time, to more than one thing at a time. Rather than lacking focus at all, we have trouble managing our focus, so we either lack focus, or we focus on something to the point of obsession, with no in-between. This obsessive focus is called *hyperfocus*. People tend to hyperfocus on things they're really interested in, which is sometimes called *fixation*. Hyperfocus is often why we don't recognize we have ADHD, and why we've done well at school and university, if that's the case.

ADHDers often have lots of thoughts and ideas but find it hard to organize them, or remember things in the short-term. All this is part of something called *executive function*.

There's more about executive function and hyperfocus below.

Executive function

Executive functions are the bosses of our brains. They help us organize our thoughts and feelings so we get things done. Problems with executive function aren't the same as lack of knowledge or ability. But problems with executive function make it more difficult for us to show what we know and can do. Managing your attention is one executive function, but there are others:

- **Working memory, better known as short-term memory**, means being able to hold information or instructions in your head and not wonder 'Where's my scarf?' while it's still on you.

- **Planning and prioritizing** means being able to get started on something and finish it, break it down into manageable chunks, judge how long it will take, and manage your time to juggle different tasks. It is also being able to organize your thoughts, and sharing a sense of what's important right now with those around you. Swedish studies of the female anatomy aren't important to most people on Christmas Day, apparently...

- **Self-monitoring** means being able to keep track of what you're doing, checking in with yourself about how it's going, and knowing when it's a good idea to switch or change plans. Spending the last money in your account on going for a drink somewhere because it reminds you of someone who hasn't spoken to you properly for years is a sign this might be a challenge for you...

- Self-monitoring also includes listening to your body and acting on what it's telling you, which is called **interoception**. This means things like being able to tell when you're hungry, thirsty or tired and take care of yourself in response. Interoception is often a challenge for ADHDers and autistic people.

- **Managing your emotions (or 'Whaaat? You mean my big feelings are part of ADHD?!')**. Although it's not yet officially part of either diagnosis, it's understood that emotional regulation is a huge part of both ADHD and autism. This means being in control of your thoughts, feelings and reactions, and reacting in a way that's seen as being in proportion to the situation.

Executive functions all work together and affect each other. For example, struggling to regulate your attention *and* emotions can lead to you thinking about, feeling or doing something uncontrollably. My editor has asked me to name an example, and I've now spent an hour trying to think of one, which is longer than I wanted to, but also a handy example! Executive functions can also cancel each other out. For example, you might have learned how to plan out your time (planning and prioritizing) but find it difficult to stick to your plans (manage your attention and self-monitor). People with ADHD struggle with a lot of executive functions, which can make adult life hard. ADHD is often treated with medication, but it's also very helpful to understand why your brain works the way it does.

Hyperfocus and fixation: The other side of ADHD

The terms hyperfocus and fixation have become common in neurodivergent spaces, and having these two words to describe my experiences is an immeasurable relief. **Hyperfocus** is, as I've mentioned already, a type of intense focus that people experience as the other side to their lack of focus. A **fixation or hyperfixation** is something specific that you hyperfocus or fixate *on*, which might be an activity or hobby, an event or a person.

Fixation is most associated with autism and what are often called 'special interests' or 'special skills' – terms I avoid as I know some autistic adults find them patronizing. But it's also experienced by people with ADHD and other types of neurodivergence who might not identify as autistic. Everyone fixates sometimes, but to neurodivergent people, fixations tend to be most intense, follow patterns more, and be more directly used as ways to relieve boredom and manage (or create...) stress in our lives.

Some fixations can last a long time, and many neurodivergent people have built careers from them. ADHDers especially might tend to cycle through lots of shorter ones. Mine have been a bit of both, ranging from the ten years I spent running a particular website to the solid day I spent researching horse riding in Ibiza. This turned into another few hours researching moving to Ibiza, before I went for the more practical option of moving to the seaside in my home country.

Fixations can be hard for others to understand or keep up with – or hard for us to understand ourselves – which can make us unnecessarily feel bad about them. Fixating *isn't* harmful in itself unless it directly harms you or someone else. The main reason any fixation can become harmful is we get so absorbed in something that we lose track of time and unintentionally struggle to take care of ourselves or others. Or we get so absorbed in part of a task we lose sight of the rest of it. Ironically enough, of all the sections in this book, the one on fixation took me the longest to write because I was fixated on it! Websites and social media platforms often mimic and help to drive fixations by showing and suggesting related content to you based on sites you visit. This is partly why social media and the internet appeal to so many ADHDers.

If you've grown up without knowing you're neurodivergent or being supported, you might also be more prone to negative fixations, like reliving traumatic events or obsessively comparing yourself to others. For obvious reasons, it's difficult for me to give my own examples of this in detail, but fixating on other people's ability to do things I find hard is one, as you'll notice throughout the book.

Hyperfocus in ADHD or autism is different from mania, paranoia or compulsions, which are part of other diagnoses, but may go together in some people.

Monotropism, a theory developed by researcher and activist Dinah Murray, explains autistic and ADHD experiences of fixation in more detail.

> For more about fixation on events, see Chapter 7. For more about fixation on people and in relationships, see Chapter 11.

The three types of ADHD

There are different ways ADHD can present. If you're diagnosed with ADHD professionally, this may or may not include your ADHD type:

1. **Predominantly hyperactive and impulsive** is what most people think of as ADHD and is most associated with boys and men. As it sounds, people with this type are active and on the go. Women and girls can be hyperactive, but our hyperactivity looks different so is often missed. I never thought greeting someone by squealing 'Hiiii!!!!' and sprinting down the pavement before going over on my ankle into a flowerbed, or being yelled at to shut up when I wouldn't stop talking, made me the same as the boy at primary school who always got into trouble for wandering around the classroom. Or for singing lines from the strange medley of hip hop and Frank Sinatra he seemed to have stuck in his head. But decades later, I realized what we had in common…

2. **Predominantly inattentive** is the under-recognized type of ADHD and is most associated with women. People with this type appear less hyperactive and tend to be dreamy and forgetful. This type used to be called 'ADD', with no H. The separate diagnosis was abolished in 1987, but like power ballads and casual sexism, it's never quite gone away.

3. **Combined type** is the most common ADHD type. People with this type have about the same amount of hyperactivity and inattention.

Hyperactive types are often found in showbusiness or prison. Inattentive types are often found in therapy rooms and on social media, sharing introvert memes. But ADHDers of all types can be found everywhere.

What ADHD is NOT
Let's consider the biggest misconceptions about ADHD.

ADHD is NOT 'laziness'
In the dedication to his book *Laziness Does Not Exist*, social psychologist Dr Devon Price (2021) writes: 'For Kim, who taught me that if a person's behaviour doesn't make sense, it's because I'm missing a piece of their context.'

I am one of the lucky ADHDers who's been described as hard-working and trying my best (or crazy/moody/annoying/incompetent…) far more often in my life than I've been described as lazy. Even so, I fume when people describe ADHDers as lazy, for two reasons. First, whether your neurodivergence is mistaken for 'laziness' or something else often comes down to other people's prejudices, and either way, it doesn't get you the right support. Second, laziness is nothing like ADHD. Often, what we describe as being lazy is either something that would be better described as a sense of entitlement (like someone dropping litter on the floor because they think mess is for others to clear up), a lack of ambition (meaning, someone is lacking in whatever ambitions we think they should have) or an occasional, temporary feeling ('I can't be bothered to wash the floor today').

Executive dysfunction in ADHD is none of these things. It's a difficulty relating thoughts to actions and a chronic feeling of *wanting or needing to do something but not being able to make yourself do it*. The parts of executive function that are easiest to describe or make into a funny meme can make it sound like laziness. The parts we tend not to describe in public, or even to our close family or best friends, look quite different.

What people call 'laziness'

- Watching TV instead of doing the housework or going for a run.
- Wanting to bunk off work early on a sunny day.
- Buying lunch one day instead of making it.
- Not doing things for other people because you don't care about other people.
- Enjoying doing nothing all day.
- Doing something fun instead of something important.

What executive dysfunction looks like

- Plugging in the hoover, then spending 15 minutes pacing the room thinking about something that happened years ago before you switch it on.
- Getting dressed for a run in the morning, then having it pointed out to you at 5pm that you haven't left the house, and wondering where the hours in between went.
- Staying at home on sunny days hoping the sun will help you get some work done.

- Spending an afternoon sending restaurant recommendations and photos of your cat to someone you've met once in real life, then realizing you still haven't replied to your best friend's text from three days ago.
- Forgetting to eat or go to the loo until you almost pass out from hunger or wet yourself.
- Eagerly volunteering to do something and then waking up every morning for weeks with a sick dread thinking about it but not being able to get started.
- Crying in despair because you're bored of doing nothing all day but can't make yourself do anything.
- Spending all day doing something which might not be necessary or even fun but is literally all you can think about.

ADHD is NOT just 'struggling to concentrate on something because it's hard or boring'

If you're dyspraxic, dyslexic or autistic, you'll find certain tasks difficult and naturally prefer to avoid them. But executive dysfunction can make it difficult to consistently enjoy the things you love as well as do the things you hate. I struggle to concentrate on spreadsheets or sewing because I find them hard. I also struggle to sit down and write without medication despite it being my job and one that I enjoy.

ADHD is NOT related to object permanence

There is a very common piece of misinformation online that ADHDers forget about things we can't see because we don't have object permanence. Object permanence is a child development term for the stage when babies are able to understand that things or people still exist even when they can't see them. All humans reach this stage at the age of around six months, so unless you're a newborn baby, it's not something you're lacking. ADHDers forget things because we lack short-term memory, and visual reminders can make things more memorable. Forgetting to call your grandma is very different to not realizing she still exists when she's out of the room.

Misconceptions about neurodivergence more generally

Here are some more myths about any or all types of neurodivergence.

Neurodivergence is NOT just 'being quirky' or 'not fitting in'
Struggling with what's expected of you can definitely be part of neurodivergence, but being someone who doesn't follow the crowd isn't a sign of neurodivergence by itself. Some neurodivergent women are happy standing out, others try their hardest to blend in, many of us do both in different situations. What makes you neurodivergent isn't just the fact that you're different but *why*. Is your look based on clothes you find easy or hard to wear because they're too difficult to put on or too likely to stain? What do you enjoy or find difficult about your life, and what do you think would be easier or harder for you if your life was different? Some people choose to be different. For neurodivergent people, difference chooses you.

Neurodivergence is NOT 'negativity' or feeling bad about yourself
If a tribe of young, female extraterrestrials came to this planet and stumbled around in the dark all night, some Instagram life

coaches would probably invite them to subscribe to their empowering newsletter instead of explain to them what a lamp is. Dyspraxia and ADHD are a brain difference. You can change the way you feel about it, or learn to work with it, but you can't change it by liking yourself, any more than you can positive-think your way out of darkness rather than switching a light on. Where self-sabotage comes into neurodivergence is that impulsivity and/or poor self-esteem from a lack of understanding and support can lead you to make choices that aren't good for you.

Neurodivergence is NOT brain damage

Neurodivergence affects the way the brain works, but it's not accurate – or in any way okay – to describe this as brain damage. Most dyspraxic people and ADHDers are dyspraxic from birth – these are what are known as developmental differences – and not because of a brain injury.

Dyspraxia and ADHD: The dream team

This book is about dyspraxia and ADHD because these types of neurodivergence are my lived experience and they often come as a pair. Scandinavian countries have been diagnosing them together for decades under the well-meant but unsexy acronym of **DAMP (Disorders of Attention, Motor Skills and Perception)**. In other countries, most people are still given a single diagnosis when they may have both. This is why attention or organizational problems are often described as being part of dyspraxia rather than ADHD and 'clumsiness' as part of ADHD rather than dyspraxia. Difficulty with short-term memory is often linked to both, as well as dyslexia, and nobody's quite sure where it comes from or how to explain it, which adds to its already-annoyingness.

Although it isn't officially part of dyspraxia or ADHD alone, everyone I know with both, like me, struggles with maths, and some people identify with **dyscalculia**, a specific difficulty with numbers. I haven't gone into dyscalculia in this book as I've never heard of an adult getting support with it. I have heard of it being recognized in schools, which is helpful to know if you're a fellow dyspraxic-ADHD maths struggler with kids, or are thinking of going back into education.

What causes dyspraxia and ADHD (and what doesn't)

Although no one is sure exactly, experts widely think that dyspraxia and ADHD are genetic, and caused by differences in how our brains handle an important chemical, dopamine. Dopamine is often described as the brain's 'reward chemical' which makes us feel pleasure, but it also controls all the executive functions I talked about earlier: motivation, planning and organizing, as well as physical coordination. In some people, dopamine gets absorbed too quickly, so there isn't consistently enough to go around and help us with all those brain functions, giving us everything we call ADHD, dyspraxia, or both.

Lots of everyday activities are known as dopamine boosters, including exercising, listening to music, eating, gaming and using social media. This is thought to be one of the reasons why ADHD is so common in online communities and the tech industry. It's not that social media causes ADHD, but ADHDers are most attracted to it because of the dopamine that comes from likes and shares. The online world is the closest thing to a world designed by and for us. Asking 'Why do so many people online have ADHD?' is a bit like asking why there are so many Manchester United supporters at a Manchester United game.

Because we don't get all the dopamine we need all of the time, ADHDers tend to prefer activities that boost dopamine fastest and make up for what we haven't got. As well as gaming and social media, these can include extreme sports, fast driving, gambling, and unfortunately, alcohol, cigarettes and street drugs. This is partly why ADHDers can have higher impulsivity and are thought to be more vulnerable to addiction.

Dyspraxic and/or physically disabled ADHDers can face a double disadvantage because exercise, which is one of the healthier ways to get dopamine faster, tends to be less accessible to us. For many ADHDers, the most effective way to manage the dopamine in our systems is through prescribed medication.

> Chapter 8 has more about how ADHD brains work and how ADHD medication works in the brain.

Most of the time, people are born with dyspraxia and/or ADHD. Although the life you lead can make dyspraxia or ADHD more challenging, there's no evidence that anything can directly make someone dyspraxic or cause ADHD which wasn't there before. Most of the things we do, like using smartphones, make our lives both a great deal harder and a great deal easier at the same time.

Final thoughts

If you didn't already, you should now know the basics of what dyspraxia and ADHD are and what they look like when you're an adult. You will have been introduced to key related terms that are used professionally and in the neurodivergent community, like executive function. The next chapter looks at some experiences you might recognize if you've lived for a long time without knowing or being supported.

> **CHAPTER 1: A QUICK RECAP**
>
> - Dyspraxia and ADHD are under-recognized in women and often look like other things: anxiety, depression, or so-called 'imposter syndrome'.
> - Dyspraxia is under-recognized as a whole compared to other types of neurodivergence and deserves to be understood in its own right. Hand-eye coordination still matters when you don't have to play sports at school anymore.
> - ADHD is about how you *manage* attention, not *pay* attention. This often makes it hard for people to recognize it in themselves.

CHAPTER 2

Self-Understanding

'So, THAT'S Why I Feel This Way...?'

There are different ways people come to learn about neurodivergence and relate it to their lives. For me and most neurodivergent people I know, there isn't one big 'wow' moment where a diagnosis falls into place, but it happens after a combination of big and small moments over time. Often, people start to understand their neurodivergence through one another, relating to the same feelings and experiences, which don't fit the textbook little-boy stereotypes.

Some feelings and experiences you might relate to if you're neurodivergent

These are a combination of my own experiences and those I come across time and time again in women. None of these alone makes someone neurodivergent or is unique to neurodivergence. But the more of these you can relate to, the more likely it is that learning about neurodivergence can help you.

You're an 'all or nothing' person

People often misunderstand that being neurodivergent means having a low ability. What it usually looks like is having *very uneven* abilities. Everyone is better at some things than others and has good and bad days. But with neurodivergence – for me, dyspraxia and ADHD – the difference between what's easier or harder, or a good and bad day, is much more dramatic. You might feel as if things seem to either come as easily to you as breathing or be far harder for you than most people, whether it's different subjects at school or tasks at work. When doing tasks, you either find it hard to concentrate on what you're doing or find it hard to think of anything else.

You are a very different person according to who you're with and what you're doing

Up to a point, it's healthy to show people different sides of yourself at different times, or treat some people in your life differently from others. You don't speak to your boss or someone you're in love with in the same way (unless they're the same person, which is a much bigger problem...). But if you're neurodivergent, you may feel that a lot of people never know the real you, or you're not even sure what the 'real' you is. You may often feel that people also either see what you can do or can't do, and are confused when they see both. Maybe you've even heard two people who know you from a different place talking about you and wondering if they're talking about the same person. This can be because of our uneven abilities, and also because of **masking**.

Masking is a term mostly used in the autistic and ADHD community, which means trying to seem more or less neurodivergent in order to fit in. This can be by deliberately hiding neurodivergent traits, like trying very hard not to fidget during a meeting, or avoiding opening a bottle in front of someone because you find it difficult. Or we can mask without realizing it. One of the ways I mask most often is hiding how good my long-term memory is, because admitting I still remember the birthdays of people I went to primary school with or the exact dates I met someone once or twice has scared away one person too many. More extreme ways of masking, like hiding feelings from someone, or putting up with sensory overload, can be really bad for our mental health, especially for long periods of time. Another type of masking which can wear us down is telling little white lies to cover up things we find difficult ('Sorry for the slow reply, my internet was down', 'I tried to call but couldn't get through...').

Because masking uses up a lot of energy, we tend to mask the most in our most conditional relationships, like at work, or when we're told to be on our best behaviour, and we feel freer to be ourselves around our closest family and friends. To those people, this can unfortunately look as if we try our hardest to please everyone else and don't care about them (or 'smarming around' other people, as I was once hurtfully accused of...).

Masking isn't the same as being deliberately manipulative, abusive or lying. The important difference between them comes from why people do them and how they feel about it. Masking is a way of coping in a world not designed for you. People who mask often lie to protect others as well as themselves and generally don't enjoy it or feel good about getting away with it. I once let a teacher think she'd lost an essay I had never handed in and felt so endlessly bad about it that I confessed and apologized to her when we met up ten years later. Masking is often about covering up difficulties which make you feel inferior to others. A person can be neurodivergent and abusive, but masking in itself won't make you abusive. Abusers have generally learned to behave that way from having it done to them or being in environments where it feels normal and acceptable, not through masking.

You find 'easy' tasks harder and 'hard' ones easier

You may have been given a so-called 'easy' task because you were young or new to something, and found it anything but easy. Or been told off for thinking something's beneath you when it was actually hard for you. On the other hand, you may be great at things others find complicated, like coming up with big ideas, or talking about things others shy away from. Maths baffled me all the way through school. At secondary school, I could do advanced questions on a practice paper, but not the simple ones designed for children younger than me. It was the same in early jobs, when I dreaded being able to use the photocopier more than being asked to write 200 interesting words about a local MP. It was difficult to say this in a way that didn't seem to give the wrong impression. Finding out I was neurodivergent was the answer I needed.

An experience that's common to dyspraxia and/or ADHD specifically is frequent accidents resulting from everyday tasks, from accidentally flooding the bathroom to opening car doors onto people by mistake (I still remember the screams...). You might equally avoid doing hands-on or practical things wherever possible in case they lead to accidents.

You seem to work harder than others to achieve the same thing, or achievements don't always seem to match your effort

Maybe you revised one subject more than any of the others put together, just to scrape through. Or you stuck at driving to get a better job, but it took you years to learn. You might also find it harder to do the things you love sometimes because it's harder to rein in your ideas. ADHDers can have difficulty with planning, organizing, short-term memory and getting started or finishing a task. It's as if something gets stuck between 'thinking' and 'doing'.

You take a lot of personality tests, and seem to get 'rare' results

Psychometric testing and so-called intelligence testing have a shady history of being used for all sorts of discrimination and there are many reasons not to take them seriously. But people who score unevenly or are told they are an unusual/'rare' type on these sorts of tests are often neurodivergent.

You've been called a lot of vague, unhelpful things

Checklists to do with dyspraxia or ADHD are about how we learn or work. Many of the signs of unrecognized ADHD in women are also about how we feel about ourselves and how others see us as people. You might have been described as intense, an overthinker, worrier, perfectionist, or too introverted/extroverted at different times. Or you might have related to an influencer who says they have 'imposter syndrome', or are 'type A', 'highly sensitive' or an 'empath'. The trouble with words like these is that they explain *what* we feel rather than *why*. They're also almost always used to make people feel better or worse than others rather than help people.

You've been treated for a mental health problem or had a lot of counselling, but it hasn't helped enough

'Maybe your problem is that you're just addicted to counselling!' said someone close to me once. From my late teens all the way through my twenties, I saw a new counsellor almost every year. Each time, I'd make the best of my handful of allocated sessions, then within a year or two, I'd be sitting in front of someone else, somewhere else, with another problem, and the old ones still unresolved. The fact that by 25 I'd had enough counselling stints to fill a CV but hadn't held down a well-paid job for more than a couple of years or had a serious relationship at all was seen as an ever-more personal failing rather than a sign I still wasn't getting the right support. I was told time and time again that the only person who could really help me was me and that there was no magic pill or super shrink. At 30, after multiple bereavements, I thankfully chose not to believe that, and instead finally went and found both those things.

Nearly every neurodivergent woman's story I've ever known follows a similar pattern of years being treated for mild-to-moderate anxiety or depression, which never goes away or gets worse enough to qualify for more help. Neurodivergence can affect the way we respond to other traumatic events in our lives, like grief and loss, or make us seem to attract drama in our relationships (see Chapter 11). ADHD can also be misdiagnosed as or go along with other mental health conditions, like bipolar, or personality disorders. There's some confusion and disagreement about whether ADHD should be described as a mental health condition in itself. Whether you think so or not, it's important to know that unrecognized ADHD can lead to mental health problems, and understand that ADHD is different from certain mental health problems. See the end of the book for links to information on and support with mental health.

People have suggested you have a 'hormonal imbalance'

Hormones are responsible for many important things in our bodies, including the way dyspraxia and/or ADHD present throughout the month. But 'hormonal imbalance' isn't a helpful way to explain this. Or in fact, a helpful term at all.

You were premature or a 'difficult' birth

If you're neurodivergent, the chances are you made an impression on the world as soon as you arrived. You might, like me, have been born early or your birth might have had complications. If you were born with other, more obvious health conditions, they were probably used to explain everything about you. If not, your parents may have felt caught between trying not to single you out and wondering whether to look for something without knowing what to look for.

You recognize traits of others in your family in yourself

My late paternal grandmother was a fine artist, well liked in the community, and known for her loyalty and generosity. She was also accident prone with no indoor voice, and when she took photos with a film camera, half had a finger over the lens or someone's arm out of shot. My mum was a hard-partying rebel who hated studying and competed with four noisy brothers for attention. It takes her half a day to leave the house, her days often end quite differently from the one planned, and her moods can be an adventure. My dad is sensitive to noise and, although good with people when he needs to be, is quite happy alone with a book. While I'm not qualified to diagnose anyone as neurodivergent, and you shouldn't make claims about any private individual in public without their consent, it's not hard to see how they produced a daughter like me. Dyspraxia, dyslexia, ADHD and autism are all thought to be at least partly genetic.

Most of the people drawn to you seem to be neurodivergent, or from other minority backgrounds

Having a very diverse group of friends could just mean you're an open-minded person and the spaces where you meet people are very diverse. But as the saying goes, 'Your vibe attracts your tribe.' If you attract a lot of people who are 'different' from others in some way, maybe there's something 'different' about you too; especially if they're the people you're closest to. You might also have found yourself weirdly attracted to someone who seems incredibly different from you on the surface, then dug deeper and realized you're actually incredibly similar. This can be because of a similar neurotype.

You have an unusual relationship with being a woman
You may have been made to feel like the 'wrong' kind of woman in certain ways. You might not like a lot of things that are stereotyped as 'male' interests, like maths or practical subjects, but also find beauty routines hard work, or never bother with them. When you were younger, you may have questioned your sexuality or gender identity as part of feeling that you didn't fit in, and different questions are coming up for you now that those have been answered.

You explain yourself to other people a lot
Probably one of the first adult words I learned was 'justify'. I was told I kept *justifying* myself. This was, of course, because I was continuously being asked to do so.

You never sleep, or your sleep patterns are wild
If your friends always text you late at night because they know you'll reply, or you schedule emails so your tutor or boss doesn't know you're working at midnight, you're a typical ADHDer.

It takes you a long time to get over difficult situations...
If you're neurodivergent, you might work through difficult feelings or traumatic experiences more slowly than others, and feel 'stuck' on them more easily. There's more about the reasons for this later in the book. Medication, therapy and life experience can all help you manage emotions, which can make life easier. However, slower emotional processing isn't a weakness.

...especially if they involve rejection or criticism
Sensitivity to rejection or criticism is one of the most common neurodivergent experiences. Given that being criticized is also one of the most common neurodivergent experiences, it's not hard to see why. As someone who's spent five years writing a

novel inspired by a time I felt rejected, it would be fair to say rejection sensitivity can affect me a lot, and like many ADHDers who have periods, it tends to be worse around that time of the month. Equally, though, there are times when I've shrugged off a rejection like a cold, and there are types of rejection I find easier to deal with than plenty of other people.

Some ADHD experts believe we're more sensitive to criticism not just because of the amount of it we're used to, but also because of the emotional dysregulation I mentioned earlier. You might have come across the term 'rejection sensitivity dysphoria' (RSD) used by ADHDers and autistic people to describe extreme sensitivity to rejection. Because how I deal with rejection can vary so much, I don't tend to use the term specifically or find it helpful to think of my rejection sensitivity as a specific disorder. I'm also iffy about the term RSD because the inventor of it (in my view) recommends a very specific, and it seems fairly inaccessible, treatment. But if you've ever struggled with feelings around rejection to the point of getting or considering professional help, understanding your neurodivergence can help you further.

Your late teens and early twenties were particularly tough

Often, the point where life with unrecognized neurodivergence starts to become seriously tricky is when you're around 16–18. There are two possible reasons for this. First, hormonal changes in women after puberty can make the challenges of dyspraxia and/or ADHD worse (see Chapter 9). It's also usually the peak time in life when you're expected to take on and balance a lot of responsibilities on your own for the very first time: from studying and working to learning to drive, starting relationships and living away from home.

In the UK, the jump from structured and guided learning to more practical work or independent study at this age is especially big, and this is often where ADHD starts to show itself most. Although adjusting to this is tough for plenty of neurotypical young people too, they tend to go through the typical milestones more quickly and easily, and find life easier as they get older. If you're a neurodivergent person without support, that teenager-y feeling of confusion might seem as if it's never gone away, and every new step seems to end in a setback rather than a move forward.

Something seems to hold you back from enjoying life
No matter how good you are at some things, or how keen you are at some things, those which don't come as naturally to you often seem to stop you getting where you want to go. You wanted to join the choir at university, but bailed out of the audition because you can't sight-read. Your friends invited you on holiday, but you pretended you couldn't go because travelling makes you too anxious. You know you'd be absolutely brilliant at one of the essential requirements on a job specification, but you'll struggle too much with another so it's not worth applying. You thought that once you got to a certain point in life, things would get easier or less overwhelming, but that hasn't happened. Over time, these 'buts' and panic episodes can add up to make you feel as if you're missing out on the life you could be living.

You were okay, but now something's changed in your life
Maybe your neurodivergence has been recognized and well supported before, or you've lived a life that's suited your neurodivergence enough without the need for a diagnosis. But now something's changed. Maybe you've lost the support of someone you love because of a breakup or bereavement. Maybe a new boss at work is impossible. And maybe when you look back on your life, it's often when things change that they get too difficult.

'Is this REALLY me...?' Dealing with doubt

Because dyspraxia and ADHD can make it harder to work with what our minds and bodies tell us, and because we're more used to being criticized or questioned, we're less likely to trust ourselves and our own instincts. Executive functions aren't fully developed until your late twenties, and ADHD symptoms are often seen as just part of being young. At university, my procrastination and late nights were hardly unusual. But my nocturnal habits didn't go unnoticed by housemates, who were also students but mostly seemed able to go to bed at times working adults went to bed, and do what they were supposed to be doing at any given time. One day, I stayed up until 5am rearranging a short paragraph for a website I ran, then went to my 9am seminar too tired to sit up and had to talk my tutor out of buying me a taxi home, a 15-minute walk away. I didn't explain anything to him, but he clearly sensed this wasn't a cause of the usual student excess. I didn't know then that this obsessive focus had a name, but I knew that spending five hours on the wording of a Contact Us page wasn't something most people did.

I can't diagnose you with dyspraxia or ADHD. What I can tell you is that *if you feel you're different from other people and it's affecting your ability to do the things you want and need to do, you're probably right.*

Of course, it's also okay not to have any doubts. If you're pretty sure you know what you're dealing with and it's the first time you've felt pretty sure of anything in your life, there's probably a reason for that too.

If you're dealing with doubts because of reactions from family and friends, see Chapter 5 on dealing with other people's reactions.

'Is this a neurodivergent thing or just a "me" thing?'

There isn't an easy or simple answer to this one, because neurodivergence isn't something temporary and easy to separate from who you are, like having a cough or a suntan. It's *part* of our personality, in the way that an ingredient is part of a cake and adding or taking away ingredients will make it look, taste and smell different. This doesn't mean that every single thing we do is entirely because of the diagnosis we have, just as there's no one ingredient in a cake that makes it a cake. As I also said in the Introduction, there are many other parts of our lives that make us who we are. What we call dyspraxia or ADHD is made up of traits, and what those traits look like is often down to those other parts of our lives, like our age and gender, when and where we grew up, and the people around us.

One example that comes to mind is fixation and anxiety. If you're a neurodivergent woman living in Canada, you're more likely to have a deep love of watching ice hockey than if you grew up in Australia, which might have led to a fascination with studying reptiles. If you're ten years younger than me, you probably don't deal with anxiety by re-watching episodes of British soaps from the 1990s online (although I can recommend it...). In short, many of the things you do are neither neurodivergent things nor 'you' things, but *both*.

The same traits or behaviours can also be helpful or unhelpful in different situations. To take another example linked to neurodivergence, someone taking risks might mean they commit crime or become a compulsive gambler, or it might mean they become a daring artist. Struggling with coordination might lead to you staying indoors and avoiding people, or it might lead to you being passionate about making design more accessible. I've done both these things in my life. This is also why I try to avoid absolute statements about traits or behaviour linked to neurodivergence. Neurodivergence is never the only reason we do something, whether it's something 'good' or 'bad'. It's often part of the explanation for why we do things. I'll give lots more examples from my experience as we go through this book. Neurodivergence doesn't make me or you tragic or gifted, kind or unkind, it makes you you. A rare human who's no less human.

Final thoughts

If this chapter describes you and your life, it's probably felt like a lot to you, especially if you're not used to recognizing yourself in other people. There's more about being kind to yourself in Chapter 7. If you don't have a professional diagnosis and are thinking about getting one, the next chapter is all about that.

CHAPTER 2: A QUICK RECAP

- There are common feelings and experiences often linked to neurodivergence, especially if you haven't had support. These can include feelings of otherness, uneven abilities, sleep patterns and family traits.
- Some people find it difficult to recognize their neurodivergence because of self-doubt. Others learn about neurodivergence and feel absolutely certain it describes them. Either is okay.
- Not everything you do is because of your neurodivergence, but it's not something you can separate from who you are.

CHAPTER 3

Should I Get Assessed Professionally?

Getting a diagnosis of dyspraxia or ADHD, or adding one diagnosis to another, is probably one of the biggest decisions you'll ever make and will probably involve some of your favourite and least favourite things at the same time. On the fun side, there's disappearing down internet rabbit holes and looking for everything you need to know about something you're interested in. On the less fun side, there's waiting, uncertainty, paperwork and sometimes money. How, when and where you're diagnosed can depend on which diagnosis you go for, where you live, work or study, your financial situation and the support you have from other people. But there are things everyone should know about diagnosis, and feelings – often mixed – that are common at the start of the journey.

Whether you're excited, or overwhelmed, or (probably) a bit of both, this chapter is a handy guide to what to think about and what to expect along the way...

'Do I need a professional diagnosis?'

A formal diagnosis is essential for some types of support. But people also often think they need a diagnosis to get certain support when that's not guaranteed, or not true. It's helpful to know when you definitely need a diagnosis and when you might not...

When you definitely need a professional diagnosis
For ADHD medications, almost anywhere
In most countries, including the UK, US and Australia, you'll need to be assessed by a doctor, usually a psychiatrist, to get a prescription for ADHD medication. In parts of Canada, if you're already diagnosed with a co-occurring condition, like dyspraxia or autism, you can be prescribed ADHD medication without needing another diagnosis.

> There's more about ADHD medication in Chapter 8.

For Disabled Students Allowance (DSA) in the UK
UK university and college students with disabilities, including mature students and postgraduates, are eligible for a grant to pay for equipment or study skills coaching to help with their course. Most universities have support staff who are aware of ADHD and dyspraxia and will be able to help you, but you'll usually need written evidence to apply.

In the US, students with disabilities may be eligible for grants, bursaries and student loan reductions (Welding, 2023). As far as I'm aware, there's no single definition of a disability, so check with your college or any college you're applying to.

For certain UK government disability benefits related to daily living and getting around

If you're dyspraxic and/or have ADHD, you might be eligible for certain benefits to help with the cost of daily living, but it's very likely you'll need medical evidence such as a formal diagnosis in order to qualify. This *doesn't* include support at work like Access to Work, or any benefits you get because you're unemployed or on a low income, which you *don't* need a formal diagnosis to claim, although a diagnosis might help with your claim (see below).

Getting a diagnosis if you live outside the UK

Healthcare varies between countries and territories, and can change over time. Always check with organizations in your country or area.

Details of all support organizations are at the end of the book.

In the Republic of Ireland: At present, adult DCD (dyspraxia) assessment services are not available through the public health system for people born before 1 June 2022. Dyspraxia in adults is usually diagnosed privately by an occupational therapist (OT). Dyspraxia Ireland can help you find your nearest OT.[1]

ADHD is diagnosed by a psychiatrist. ADHD Ireland's website has a list of clinicians who diagnose adults.[2]

In the US: Sadly, and surprisingly, adult dyspraxia is

---

[1] www.dyspraxia.ie/Adults-with-Dyspraxia-DCD
[2] https://adhdireland.ie/adhd-irelands-list-of-clinicians

little-known in the US so adult diagnosis is rare. Dyspraxia Foundation USA may be able to advise you on getting a diagnosis. Jenny Hollander (2022), a dyspraxic journalist originally from the UK who now lives in the US, has written about the frustration of dyspraxia being poorly understood in the US.

ADHD is much better known and is recognized as a disability under the Americans with Disabilities Act and by the Centers for Disease Control and Prevention (CDC). The first step towards an adult ADHD diagnosis is to talk to a primary physician or mental health provider.

In Canada: Dyspraxia in adults is usually diagnosed by a neurologist. Like all countries, much of their research into dyspraxia is centred around children. However, CanChild,[3] a Canadian website, has the most visible and well-organized dyspraxia research I've seen from any country, so it's worth a visit for anyone exploring dyspraxia, especially if you're the parent of a dyspraxic child.

ADHD is diagnosed by a psychiatrist or psychologist, and you should contact your primary health provider first.

In Australia and New Zealand: Both countries have their own dyspraxia organizations for children and adults. Their contact details are at the end of the book.

As in other countries, ADHD in adults is diagnosed by a psychiatrist.

In South East Asia: Some medications that are common in other countries are illegal in Japan, including certain stimulants used to treat ADHD. This also means you can't

---

[3] www.canchild.ca

> bring them into the country, for example if you're on holiday or studying abroad. However, the ban largely applies to short-acting stimulants. Some long-acting stimulants have recently been made legal and can be prescribed or brought into the country. Visit the Japanese Health Ministry's website for more information.[4]

When a professional diagnosis might be helpful

For your confidence

Having 'proof' of a diagnosis can make you feel more comfortable in the world, especially around people in authority, and in situations where what you get depends on who you see and what mood they're in.

You were diagnosed as a child, and it was never explained to you properly

This is quite likely if you're in your twenties or older. Along with the rest of this book, an adult assessment can help you make sense of your diagnosis in a grown-up way.

You have a diagnosis that hasn't given you all the answers or support you need

If you've been diagnosed with dyspraxia, the most common reason for seeking an ADHD diagnosis is to try medication. If you have an ADHD diagnosis, being diagnosed with dyspraxia is less likely to get you extra support, but should help you understand parts of yourself an ADHD diagnosis won't reach.

---

[4] www.mhlw.go.jp/english/policy/health-medical/pharmaceuticals/01.html

If you're claiming benefits because you're unemployed or on a low income

If you're unemployed, the Job Centre should take dyspraxia and ADHD into consideration when drawing up your jobseeker's agreement, and let you apply for the jobs you're most able to do. You shouldn't need a formal diagnosis for this. But as the words 'should' and 'shouldn't' don't always matter to who you see, proof of anything is helpful to have.

For some local disability schemes

Some local authorities run support schemes for things like public transport, which might ask for proof of your disability. Sending a copy of your diagnosis document can be handier than finding and paying someone to write a letter.

For taking part in research

If you follow a lot of neurodiversity-related accounts online, you'll often see callouts offering you chocolate and vouchers for taking part in academic studies. For various reasons they might specify they're looking for people either with or without a formal diagnosis.

Where you *don't* need a professional diagnosis
To read the rest of this book

This chapter is about diagnosis because that's the first reason most people pick up a book on neurodiversity. Apart from the sections on medication, you don't need a diagnosis for anything else.

In the UK, to apply for support at work under the Equality Act

A good diagnostic report can help your employer understand more about dyspraxia or ADHD. But unlike at school and university, you don't legally need written evidence to get support.

Dyspraxia and ADHD are recognized as disabilities under the Equality Act, which doesn't say you need a diagnosis to be covered. Access to Work is a UK government grant available to disabled people for coaching or equipment at work and, in some cases, travel to and from work or essential work travel. Although the paperwork involved isn't exactly neurodiversity-friendly, you don't need a formal diagnosis to apply. I'm not aware of anything directly equivalent to Access to Work outside the UK, but in the US and most other countries, employers are required by law to make reasonable adjustments for disabled employees (Americans with Disabilities Act 1990). As far as I'm aware, you don't need a diagnosis for this, although it may help your employer to give you the right support.

To show that your dyspraxia or ADHD hasn't gone away since you were little
The only good reason to be re-assessed is that your needs aren't being met or you want to understand your diagnosis better. You shouldn't need to prove to anyone that you haven't turned from a dyspraxic child into an Olympic figure skater.

Less positive reasons for being diagnosed
You're being pushed into it
No one should use your diagnosis to harm or punish you. If they do, the best thing a diagnosis can do for you is to help to keep you away from them.

To bring someone closer to you than they want to be
A diagnosis can help people who care about you understand you better. But if someone doesn't care as much about you as you'd like them to, explaining your brain to them probably won't change that.

Myths about diagnosis

You can't get an adult diagnosis unless you pay for it. There's no point in even trying
It's unlikely to be quick and easy, that's for sure. But it's not impossible. And no one is better made for digging around in corners of the internet than we are. If a diagnosis feels helpful to you, nothing should stop you from trying.

You can't trust a private diagnosis. Anyone will get diagnosed if they pay for it
A diagnosis isn't something you 'order' like a takeaway, or something a doctor tries to sell you like exorbitant skincare ranges. Specialists usually do a mixture of private and NHS work. They don't get paid more for diagnosing any Random Joe who walks past, and no medical professional wants to waste time when they could be helping people who need help. All diagnostic centres use pre-assessment questionnaires and only assess people who are likely to get a diagnosis.

You should feel bad about paying for a private diagnosis
A pop-up cinema built on a bulldozed nature reserve is something you should feel bad about paying for; a diagnosis which can save lives is not.

Your family or partner have to agree for you to get a diagnosis
A diagnosis should never depend on this. Any assessment will ask you questions about your life history and relationships with other people, and the person assessing you might ask to speak to someone who knew you well has a child, or who knows you well now. But any sensible professional should understand that not

everybody has parents who are alive, helpful or good at talking to doctors, and not every woman in her twenties is in a relationship with someone who's interested in how her brain works.

If there aren't many people close to you because of trauma or because you find relationships hard, this should support your case. Old school reports can be helpful if you have them, but it shouldn't matter if you don't, and anyone who's surprised you don't probably shouldn't be diagnosing people with organizational problems. I wasn't asked for them at all when I got my dyspraxia diagnosis, and was told they were optional for my second assessment. I told the doctor I couldn't remember where they were, but that I still remember the top line of the one from my first teacher in 1989: 'Maxine is an intelligent but rather dreamy child' (Thanks, Mrs Haines!). I think he'd got the picture well enough by then, but it made him smile.

A diagnosis means you'll be registered disabled and discriminated against

There is no such thing as being 'registered disabled' in the UK, or anywhere else as far as I know. 'Registered disabled' is a misleading and outdated term which comes from having to register for a disabled parking permit. People of a certain age and some reporters who should know better still use it in ways they shouldn't, especially as a euphemism for people claiming disability benefits or who can't work because of a disability. It's problematic because it implies that any disabled person who isn't on the 'register' (or anyone who is but doesn't look disabled enough) is lying. It also tells you nothing in itself about what someone's needs are. In the UK, if someone says they're 'registered disabled', it could mean any number of things.

Almost every country has laws that are designed to protect you from discrimination if you have a disability. In the UK, dyspraxia, ADHD and autism are considered disabilities under the

Equality Act. No law is perfect (which is a whole other book), but any diagnosis gives you more legal rights than none.

A diagnosis means you're holding yourself back or 'letting it define you'
Dyspraxia and ADHD define me. Being a woman born in June also defines me, but nobody ever tells me not to let that 'define' me when I post photos of myself on the beach, or mention my birthday. When people tell someone not to be 'defined' by something, they sometimes mean: 'Don't mention something that makes me feel awkward.'

What people may also mean by 'Don't let it define you' is 'Try not to become too fixated on bad things that have happened to you or the way others have treated you', which is good advice. But the most important reason why is to make yourself feel better, not because it makes someone else feel better.

'Where do I go for a professional diagnosis?'

Where to go for a diagnosis will depend on which diagnosis you're looking for.

ADHD in adults is usually diagnosed by a psychiatrist, who can prescribe medication. Other professionals like psychologists, counsellors and coaches can assess you for ADHD, but you'll need another assessment from a psychiatrist if you want to try medication.

Dyspraxia is usually diagnosed by a psychologist or neurologist. Unlike ADHD and autism, there is no official way of being diagnosed on the National Health Service (NHS). But as a dyspraxia assessment is usually shorter than an autism or ADHD assessment and doesn't involve medication, it's often cheaper or easier to fund, especially if it's done through work or study (more on that later).

'Whole-person' assessments, which look for all types of neurodivergence together at once rather than single assessments, are becoming more common, and it is hoped that these will become the norm eventually. At the moment, they're usually non-medical assessments offered by neurodivergence coaching or training firms. But any dyspraxia or ADHD specialist should understand that neurodivergent conditions are more likely to go together than travel alone.

In the UK, depending on which you go for, there are various main routes to a professional diagnosis:

- **Your local NHS Adult ADHD Service:** Most areas will have an NHS diagnostic centre for adult ADHD. Some are for both ADHD and autism. You'll need a referral from a GP. Waiting times vary depending on where you live, and can be anything from a few weeks to five years.

- **Your local Community Mental Health Team:** NHS mental health teams carry out ADHD assessments where there isn't an adult ADHD service in the area. However, in some areas you'll need to be in treatment with them for a mental health condition.

- **Private clinics which accept NHS patients, or the 'Right to Choose' route:** This is often the easiest way to be diagnosed if you don't want to pay or wait. In England, under what's known as 'Right to Choose', you can ask your GP for an NHS referral, even if there's an NHS Adult ADHD service in your area. It's also your best option if there isn't one. Adult ADHD groups on social media will have information about the best-known providers in the UK. There are also dyspraxia clinics in the UK which offer this.

- **Your university, college or employer:** Many dyspraxic adults are diagnosed in higher education or at work, by an educational or work psychologist. Universities and colleges sometimes pay for a diagnosis for students from low-income backgrounds. If you're working and you feel a diagnosis would help you in your job, your employer should also cover part or all of the assessment cost. Work or study-based assessments are sometimes helpful for ADHD, but you'll have to go to a psychiatrist separately for medication. You can apply for Access to Work assessment for support at work without any diagnosis.

- **Small charities, support organizations and large crowdfunders:** Charities may offer neurodiversity assessments for free for people who meet certain criteria (for example, if you're unemployed, or under 25). Some also offer grants for people 'in need' which can be used to help cover the cost. There are peer groups that support disabled and neurodiverse adults from other marginalized groups and organize crowdfunds for diagnosis, which are often shared on social media.

- **Private ADHD or dyspraxia clinics:** Going private is expensive and unaffordable for many. But if you possibly can, it means you'll have less of a wait and can choose who you see.

Getting a referral from a doctor or professional

For NHS treatment in the UK, you'll need a referral from your

GP. This might be the first time you've spoken to anyone outside your family, or anyone at all. To make it easier, make a specific appointment with your GP.

Make a dedicated appointment

- It's best to see your GP to talk about ADHD or dyspraxia, rather than try and tag it on when you're there for something else.
- Ask if there's a doctor at the surgery with any experience of referring people for ADHD, dyspraxia or autism assessments. Sadly, GPs don't tend in my view to know as much as they should – and do not receive sufficient training – about neurodivergence. But some surgeries have colleagues who are trained or more experienced in dealing with certain issues, and awareness is growing. If you live in a town with more people than sheep, they may have at least referred someone before.
- Fill out some screening questionnaires and bring the results with you. The Adult ADHD Self-Report Scale (ASRS v1.1)[5] is the most common screening tool and is free to download and print or email. For dyspraxia, you can download a self-test from Dyspraxia UK.[6]
- Take some notes in with you too if it'll help you, and any other helpful written information you can find. Don't force yourself to try and wing it and then beat yourself up for going blank or forgetting something.

---

5   https://add.org/wp-content/uploads/2015/03/adhd-questionnaire-ASRS111.pdf
6   https://dyspraxiauk.com/adults

You can explain to the doctor that finding it difficult to organize your thoughts is part of the condition. If you've read articles online that you can relate to about dyspraxia or ADHD in women, save them onto your phone or tablet where you can refer to them, or ask the surgery if you can email them over before your appointment. You can also use any of the information in this book.

- Know where you want to be referred to. If there's no one experienced in referrals at the surgery, it's best to hit the internet and find out what NHS services there are in your area before your appointment. My GP didn't know about my local NHS ADHD service and referred me to the Community Mental Health Team, who sent it straight back as I wasn't a patient of theirs. If you're going for 'Right to Choose' to avoid a long waiting list, you may have to do a bit of explaining and be as polite but firm as you can. It might help to say you're coming up to a big change in your life, or thinking of moving house, and can't wait. The clinic should have information about referrals for NHS patients. Take as much with you as you can find.

- If your GP won't listen, consider complaining to the practice. Most GPs mean well and will at least try and be helpful, but outdated myths still do the rounds. If you see someone who thinks you can't have ADHD because you've got a degree, or you're not a little boy, send a strong email to the surgery and tell them to read the National Institute for Health and Care Excellence (NICE) guidelines.

Things to know about assessments

Before your assessment
Cost
A private dyspraxia or ADHD assessment can cost anything between £300 and £1000 (USD $375–1250). There are also added costs involved in ADHD medication, so if you're scraping together every penny, it's important to budget for these too.

> See Chapter 8 for everything you need to know about medication.

Timing
The way assessments are organized can vary from place to place, so it's good to know what the procedure is for wherever you're going. Will the assessment happen on one day, or will it be split into two or three sessions? Will you be told on the day, or will you have to wait for the diagnostic report to find out? How long will that take? If you want to try ADHD medication, you should have plenty of time to go through your options and not be rushed through it after you've spent an hour or two being assessed.

Whether you'd prefer to be assessed online or in person
Many people find online assessments more practical than in-person ones and most ADHD and autism clinics now offer them. For dyspraxia, an in-person assessment can be more helpful as it will be easier for the assessor to see how you move and interact in a space. Either way, letting the assessor know about your communication preferences can help them accommodate you and also support your diagnosis. For example, if video calls are easier

for you than meeting in person, or you prefer one video-calling platform over another, say so and try to explain why. Or tell them about video-calling features that annoy you, like forgetting when you're muted or unmuted on a call, which can be a sign of short-term memory problems.

Whether you'd prefer to be assessed by a woman
An assessment shouldn't be traumatic, but if there's trauma in your life history, talking to a woman might make you feel safer. If you have periods, you might also find it more helpful to be assessed by someone who knows what it's like to have them. This is especially true for ADHD, where female hormones can affect the way medication works. If you belong to another marginalized group, you may find an assessor who relates to this helpful.

> There's lots more in Chapter 9 about living with dyspraxia, ADHD and a woman's body.

What else is going on in your life right now
If you're struggling with something else, such as a bereavement or breakup, be aware you're adding something else to your plate and what that might mean. Equally, though, don't worry too much about 'The Right Time'. Times when we feel most overwhelmed are often the very times we're more likely to look for a diagnosis.

Anything you need to send before your assessment, or have with you
They should give you time to gather anything you might need, or explain why if that's not possible.

How you'll get there, if your assessment is in person
Getting a diagnosis can bring up a lot of feelings and you probably want to make the journey as easy as possible. Travel with someone else or let someone else know where you're going if you can and if it will help. If you're travelling a long way to an assessment, letting the clinic know might also help you avoid a wasted journey or too many appointments.

What comes after your assessment
'Aftercare' can vary, and for ADHD medication, it's really important. After the assessment, you'll be given a diagnostic report. They might be able to show you a sample beforehand as an idea of what to expect. Even if you're not being prescribed medication, ask if you can get in touch with the assessor later to ask about anything in the report you don't understand.

During your assessment
Dyspraxia
Educational and workplace psychologists use something called the Wechsler Adult Intelligence Scale (WAIS) to diagnose dyspraxia. This compares your verbal IQ (how well you read, write and spell) to your non-verbal IQ (your coordination and spatial skills). It's controversial and can look pretty disheartening, especially when used on its own.

Occupational therapists or neurologists who diagnose dyspraxia in adults will have different tests which will usually look at your coordination and balance.

ADHD
An ADHD assessment can be done in one day and usually lasts around two hours. But depending on where you're diagnosed and who by, it might be in two or three parts with more than one appointment, especially for ADHD if you're trying medication.

You'll probably have been asked to fill out some forms in advance, usually a pre-assessment screening and some information about yourself. If not, you might be asked to do this first thing, or while you're waiting if it's an in-person assessment. It shouldn't take long.

The assessor will ask questions about your life, including your family background, school and work history. They might start with your childhood and work forwards, or start from now and work backwards. They'll probably use a mixture of their own words ('Tell me more about some of your problems...') and formal questionnaires like DIVA (Diagnostic Interview for ADHD in Adults) or Conners' Rating Scale for ADHD. Your assessor might also talk about the *Diagnostic and Statistical Manual of Mental Disorders*, fifth edition (DSM-5), the Bible of psychiatry, which lists the diagnostic criteria for ADHD. For an in-person assessment, the assessor might also do some video-game-style tasks to test your concentration and memory.

Other ways to get the most from your assessment

Book it when you're not near your period if you can
But don't worry if you can't, or if you get your dates wrong and have to struggle through an assessment while your premenstrual syndrome (PMS) rages or your uterus tries to kill you – it'll only support your diagnosis if you mention it!

Tell them about your bad days
When you're used to hiding your difficulties, the hardest thing to remember about an assessment is that you're there because of them. Even people who talk about their brains for a living struggle to talk about *everything* that goes on in them. But a diagnosis is a

medical decision, and medical decisions are made based on *what you can't do, avoid doing, or what takes you more effort than others to do*. They're also based on things that upset you, like difficult relationships, or obsessions that rule your life. The assessor might help you break things down into specifics. For example, if you say 'I get lost quite a lot' or 'I tend to put things off', they might ask you 'How often is a lot?' or 'Tell me more about what that looks like'. Being specific might sound silly, scary or painful. But the assessor has to know you're struggling to be able to help you.

But don't be afraid to talk about the things you love

Telling someone what you're passionate about can also help with a diagnosis. Tell the assessor about times you've found it hard to focus on anything else because you're so into an interest; or found it hard to focus on something even though you've really, really wanted to.

Try not to worry if you can't do a task, or answer a question

Some of them will be designed to show up difficulties and they will be expecting you to find them hard. This is especially likely if you're being assessed for dyspraxia.

Ask for a separate medication appointment if you need to

Assessments often overrun. If at the end of an ADHD assessment there isn't enough time to discuss medication, you should be offered a separate appointment without having to pay or wait. Medication is an important decision, not something to be rattled through at the end.

Mention any other neurodivergent conditions you've been diagnosed with

A dyslexia or autism diagnosis will support an ADHD or dyspraxia diagnosis. If you have diagnostic reports, bring them with you, even if you were diagnosed as a child.

Have a tissue handy
My dyspraxia assessment at university left me a mixture of numb, tired and tested out. Near the end of my ADHD assessment, I sobbed like a girl, despite being 15 years older and having spent 15 years in the world of neurodivergence. Feeling teary during an assessment is normal and healthy, and it doesn't matter how emotionally prepared you are.

By the end of your assessment, the assessor should have given you some inkling of what their diagnosis will be. They'll confirm this in a diagnostic report, which will probably be emailed to you anything from a week to two months later, depending on their workload.

'What if I don't get a diagnosis?'

You probably will, but if not, it doesn't mean you're 'wrong'
Most people who are assessed for dyspraxia, ADHD or any other neurodivergent condition get their diagnosis. If you've spent time and money on this book and on an assessment, it's extremely likely you will too. But if I told you 99.8% of people assessed for ADHD worldwide get a diagnosis, you'd still worry about being in the 0.2%. I could tell you that 100% of dyspraxia assessments end in a diagnosis, and you'd worry about being the first not to get one. I know this because I live with an anxious brain and that's how anxious brains work. So, as my brain was fond of saying to me in double maths, forget numbers...

If someone isn't diagnosed after an assessment, there may be a number of reasons.

They didn't ask to be diagnosed, or have enough time to explain their problems
Sometimes GPs are too busy to fully listen to someone with a very vague symptom, and just whack it into a computer and send

a referral letter to one of the top search results to show they've done something.

They weren't screened before being assessed
To save time for everyone, diagnostic centres should make you a brief appointment and/or ask you to fill out a standard, short screening questionnaire, like the ASRS v1.1 for Adult ADHD, to check you're likely enough to get a diagnosis before they book you in for a full assessment. Ideally, they should do this well before your assessment appointment rather than on the day, but they might give it to you at the beginning of the assessment or while you're waiting instead. If this happens and you don't score highly enough, they might not carry on with the assessment. If you've paid them anything, you should be entitled to some money back.

The assessor wasn't trained to diagnose, or their knowledge is stuck in a time warp
A duty psychiatrist told my friend she couldn't have ADHD because she has a PhD and could describe how to make a cup of tea. Another friend was told she wasn't autistic because of outdated studies done on men and boys. Being a health professional doesn't make someone good at diagnosing everything, any more than being a professional writer means I can write about anything. If an assessor clearly has absolutely no idea what they're talking about, you have every right to ignore their opinion, or ask for another one.

The assessor feels that a diagnosis they already have explains enough
If you have a diagnosis of something else, an assessor could feel that the existing diagnosis needs to be supported or explained to you better rather than added to. You don't have to agree.

The assessment scores were borderline
You might not get a diagnosis because you scored close to the diagnostic threshold but not 'over the line', or you met some of the assessment criteria but not enough. This is the most usual reason for not getting a diagnosis after an assessment. But as I said in the Introduction, 'borderline' scores are still likely to mean there's something worth looking into, and definitely doesn't mean you don't need or deserve support.

It's hard to tell different types of neurodivergence apart
The way that dyspraxia, ADHD and autism go together and overlap can make it hard to diagnose someone, even for experienced professionals. **Not getting a diagnosis doesn't mean there's nothing to diagnose** and can often mean there's more to you than one person can see. Some people have lots of needs but not enough fall under any one label to get any diagnosis.

Whatever happens after an assessment, the journey starts with you wanting to understand yourself better, and that's always a good thing.

'What about self-diagnosis?' (Spoiler: Yes, it's absolutely fine)

A professional diagnosis often takes time and patience or costs money; sometimes all three. As an undiagnosed dyspraxic or ADHD woman, they are exactly the three things you're least likely to have. A self-diagnosis doesn't mean someone's dyspraxia or ADHD is 'milder' or they need less help; in fact, it may mean they need more. Remember:

- **Everyone is self-diagnosed:** Anything new you ever learn about yourself comes from you, even if it includes someone else's opinion. When I was a young arts writer and used to follow actors and musicians a lot, I noticed that the more interesting and insightful interviews with them, whatever their sexuality, were often done by LGBTQIA+ publications, whereas the ones in mainstream women's magazines were empty and boring. I mulled this over with a very wise friend, who said, 'Well, I suppose it takes some depth and insight to know you're gay in the first place.' Self-diagnosis doesn't mean you've taken a shortcut; it means you've already done most of the work.

- **A diagnosis is meant to help you, not test you:** Being diagnosed is not an exam, or your driving theory, or a video game. Whether it comes from you or someone else, the most important thing any diagnosis should do is give you the answers you need when you need them. In 2005, I needed to understand why my brain worked differently and a professional diagnosis seemed the only way of finding out. I didn't go to the assessment expecting the answer would be dyspraxia, or even expect to be given a name. Neurodivergence in women was hardly talked about and dialup internet still existed. Fifteen years later, an ADHD diagnosis with a prescription confirmed what my experiences in the world of neurodivergence and my relationship with Twitter (now known as X) had already told me.

- **Most of the neurodivergent community accepts self-diagnosis:** Thankfully, there's more understanding in the world than there is nasty gatekeeping. If you're worried about how others will react to a diagnosis, there's more about this in the next chapter.

- **Knowing something for yourself can be easier than hearing it from someone else:** Any professional diagnosis, no matter how well explained or strengths led, will involve talking to a stranger about things you find hard, then hearing them agree with you. This might be something you're not ready for, or you'll never be ready for, and that's okay.

'Why is there so much confusion between different types of neurodivergence? How do I know which I am?'

Whether certain traits belong to dyspraxia, ADHD or autism can lead to more discussion and arguments in online communities than anything else. Because people often have traits associated with several neurodivergent conditions, but the conditions are usually assessed separately, people tend to have had one diagnosis and either think of all their neurodivergent traits as being part of that condition, or be left wondering if they need several more assessments. Charities and other supportive organizations are usually created and funded to support single conditions, but people who most need their help often have co-occurring needs, so they sometimes try to get around this by stretching the definition of 'their' condition. Although this is well meaning, it can be confusing and actually lead to people ending up with less understanding or support. This has especially happened with dyspraxia in the UK, as I mentioned in the first chapter.

Another possible reason for the confusion is that sometimes neurodivergent people can have the same experiences but for different reasons, and a different diagnosis might be right for you depending on which apply. Dropping and spilling things often can be a sign of coordination problems, concentration problems, or both. Making eye contact might be difficult for you because you find it distracting, you forget what your body's doing, or you find it physically painful. Some experiences, like fixation, are now understood to be common to both autism and ADHD. Others, like sensitivity to being rejected or criticized, are common to all types of neurodivergence but aren't mentioned in any of the diagnostic criteria, so they don't 'officially' belong to any diagnosis.

Specific labels matter most where they're needed for the most specific types of support, like medication. The wrong label might give people the wrong idea about what you can and can't do, which is why dyspraxics who are great readers and spellers hate dyspraxia being confused with dyslexia. On the other hand, fixating on what to label something is less helpful if it makes little difference to the support you get, or if it confuses you so much that it stops you looking for support at all.

The world would be a much simpler place if everyone could find out about and be assessed for all types of neurodivergence at the same time. One day, neuroscientists will hopefully find out and agree on exactly how what we now call dyspraxia, ADHD and autism are biologically related. Until then, assuming you don't have the time, energy or money for multiple assessments, deciding which label suits you best will probably come down to which traits are having the most impact on your life and which is the easiest to be assessed for where you live.

> There's a list of related conditions and experiences at the end of the book, with a list of further reading, and links to information and support.

Final thoughts

I hope that this chapter has cut through some of the jumble of information about diagnosis and support. If you're still confused, remember, you don't need any professional diagnosis to read the rest of this book.

CHAPTER 3: A QUICK RECAP

- Getting a professional diagnosis can be difficult but doesn't have to be. You can get it cheaper if you're prepared to search and wait. A diagnosis is just as legitimate whether it's in-person or online, and whether you pay or not.
- You might not need a professional diagnosis to get certain support. But it's always worth getting one if it feels important to you.
- You don't need your family's approval to be diagnosed as an adult, or anybody else's.
- A diagnosis from a woman can be more helpful for some women especially for ADHD medication, which interacts with female hormones, or if you live with trauma.
- Professional and self-diagnosis are both just as valid. You might gain confidence from having that bit of paper, or you might just need the knowledge, and that's fine too. The point of a diagnosis is to understand yourself, not prove yourself.

CHAPTER 4

'So This is Me! What Now?'

'Coming Out' as Neurodivergent

So, you're neurodivergent! Welcome to the club! Of course, there isn't really a club with a welcoming committee, rules or an instruction manual. What's both scary and brilliant about being diagnosed as an adult is exactly what's scary and brilliant about *being* an adult: **How you decide to live your life afterwards is up to you.** Children who are diagnosed will usually have parents or teachers to decide what happens next. You get to decide those things for yourself. You get to find out as much or as little about your diagnosis as you want, unlike children, who are usually told what people think they can handle. And when you ask, people are more likely to tell you the truth.

What's less great about recognizing your neurodivergence as an adult is it can feel as though no one really cares. If you're recently diagnosed, whether by yourself or someone else, or just wondering about how you and your existing diagnosis fit into the grand scheme of things, then this chapter is your metaphorical helping hand. Over the next two chapters, you'll learn how to talk to people about your neurodivergence, and what to do if it doesn't go as well as you'd hoped.

'Is it normal to feel this way?' Feeling your feelings about being neurodivergent

There is no 'right' or 'wrong' way to feel about finding out you're neurodivergent, and you're likely to have strong or mixed feelings. In the last chapter, I mentioned that some things can make getting a diagnosis easier or harder, like what else is happening in your life and the relationship you have with people around you. These things can also affect the way you feel afterwards. One of the most important things you can do now is to let yourself feel your feelings, whatever they are. Below, in no particular order, are some feelings that are common soon after a diagnosis, and beyond. Some are common to anyone going through a big life change, even for the most neurotypical person. But being neurodivergent affects the way we process emotions, which can make big feelings even more intense, and can mean it takes a long time for us to work through them.

Relief
The feeling of having an answer can be a massive relief, especially if you've waited a long time or spent money on being assessed, or previously had a diagnosis that was inaccurate or incomplete.

Happiness
You may feel that being neurodivergent has helped to bring you some of the things and people you love most. The intensity of that love can be incredibly special. Finding out you're neurodivergent can also make it easier for you to enjoy the things you love. I always wrote to make sense of the world. However,

living in a world that didn't make sense to me, combined with my organizational problems, also meant I struggled to actually sit down and write. Finding the help I needed to focus on my writing and organize my thoughts has helped me do more of what makes me happy.

Confusion and overwhelm
Whichever way you go about it, finding out that you're neurodivergent can be a lot to take in. I went into my dyspraxia assessment hoping to find the reason why I struggled with maths and came out with a report which didn't particularly explain why, but instead seemed to describe why I struggled with almost everything. It took me four or five years to fully take in my first diagnosis and another four or five to realize that some of my difficulties were better explained and supported with a second diagnosis. No matter how sure you are that you're neurodivergent, or which type of neurodivergence you are, don't worry if it takes time to feel anything at all.

Remembering people or events you haven't thought about in years
A diagnosis can bring back all kinds of memories, good, bad or a bit of both. These might show up in your everyday life, or in dreams. A persistent childhood memory I've had while writing this book which perfectly sums up neurodivergence is of when a ten-year-old me eagerly organized a petition to save a tree and then wrote to the council about it, forgetting to include the petition.

Anger and regrets
Positivity and new-found freedom can't always make up for the feelings that come with years of being unsupported and

misunderstood. There might be things you wish you'd done, or feel there are things people in your life could have done differently.

Going over and over the same thing (also called 'ruminating')

You may have already noticed this is something you do a lot. It's something neurodivergent people tend to do a lot!

Feeling a lot more or less sociable

You might feel excited to meet new people, or want to hide under the duvet, or swing between the two extremes even more dramatically than usual.

Noticing your neurodivergence more or feeling as if you're 'more neurodivergent'

You dropped something? Ooh, dyspraxic moment! Forgot something? Ooh, ADHD moment! Binge-watched an entire TV series in one weekend and then spent hours reading about it? That'll be the hyperfixation! Noticing your traits after a diagnosis is really common. Other people you tell may notice them too.

As well as having names for feelings you couldn't name, you might be aware of what's going on in your body too. But you might have unknowingly developed traumatic reactions to certain critical words or phrases, and you might notice these more after being assessed, or at particular times in your life.

'So what do I do now?'

Depending on how you're feeling after a diagnosis, you might feel like doing:

- **Everything!** The moment you officially 'know' or decide for yourself can make you excited to find out everything you can about being neurodivergent.

- **Nothing!** If all you want to do is forget about it for a while, or even a long time, that's also completely normal and okay. If someone else has recommended this book to help you on your journey, I'm really glad. But it's important you do things at your own pace, so don't let anyone put pressure on you. This book, and a whole community, will still be here for you whenever you're ready.

- **Both!** Switching or feeling stuck between embracing your neurodivergence and feeling overwhelmed is possibly the most common experience to have while you're learning about it.

Some specific things you might want to do when you're learning about neurodivergence:

- **Meet people like you (if you haven't already):** Most neurodivergent people I know say that finding other neurodivergent people who 'get it' has made the biggest difference to their life, and I agree. Technology (widely built by neurodivergent people...) thankfully makes it possible to connect with neurodivergent people all over the world. Meeting other people who are open about their neurodivergence is increasingly the reason people find out about their neurodivergence later in life. There's more about neurodivergent communities in Chapter 6 on story sharing, and links to further reading at the end of the book.

- **Create content or appear in the media:** Creating content on social media can be a really positive way of getting to know people. There are some things to think carefully about too. There's more about creating content and story sharing in Chapter 6.

- **Try new things:** Having the words to explain who you are can open you up to lots of new experiences which might not have felt open to you before. If you're dyspraxic, it might be something practical or sporty. For any type of neurodivergence, it might be travel or moving somewhere new. You'll see some of my own examples throughout the rest of the book.

- **Look for support at work:** Although this isn't a book about careers, there's information about talking to your employer later in this chapter.

Talking to people in your life about neurodivergence

There are several reasons you might want to tell others about your neurodivergence:

- You need support.
- Something about them has reminded you of neurodivergence, or made you think they'd be interested.
- You think someone might be neurodivergent.
- You feel you've been misunderstood.

Or, potentially most of all:

- It's interesting, and it's what's in your head right now!

Deciding who to tell, when and how

Before I knew I was neurodivergent, I had spent years feeling like an outsider and being told there was something odd about me people could smell but not name, like sniffer dogs at airports. Finding out about being dyspraxic meant finally having a way to explain me to other people. I told everyone I met in every imaginable way, including:

- Launching into an essay about my diagnosis during a mundane text conversation with a bloke I fancied who'd gone to the loo and came back baffled.
- Ending up ranting about someone else's bad reaction to my diagnosis to a stranger who'd casually started chatting to me at an induction evening.
- Handing a printed-out list of dyspraxic traits – the pre-smartphone equivalent of pulling up something on your screen in the pub, only, more effort – to someone I hadn't seen for a year who'd just finished work and quite recently had a baby. And who, strangely enough, was more interested in talking about both these things than about my brain.

A few years later, I started writing and speaking about neurodivergence as part of my work, partly as a way to make talking to new people about it easier. Later, I came to understand how the urge to explain myself and my neurodivergence to other people was linked to neurodivergence itself. Being misread as shy or antisocial had left me feeling I had to be an open book in order to be liked. Meanwhile, I fixated on things I was interested in, which made me want to talk about them a lot, and being misunderstood had become a fixation. Many neurodivergent women I know have felt similarly. But what I'd also like to have been told in my first couple of years as an 'out' dyspraxic is this:

- You don't have to explain yourself to everyone in detail all the time.
- You don't have to answer any question you don't want to.

We often talk or hear about consent when it comes to our bodies and personal space. We're told that no one has a right to sex with us, or we can wear a badge or sticker to let people at an event know we'd rather not be touched or be photographed. But quite often, we feel the opposite of this when it comes to talking about ourselves. And we live in a world where people often think they have the right to know what everyone else is thinking and doing all the time. Of course, being authentic and open about your feelings is a healthy thing, and words like 'oversharing' which are often used to shame us for being open with our thoughts are just as nasty as the words which are used to shame us for being open with our bodies.

But just like you don't owe anyone physical intimacy, or photos of your body, you don't owe anyone emotional intimacy either. That includes information about your neurodivergence, or about anything else. Neurodivergence is never something you should be made to feel bad about or hide from people. But it's also okay not to mention it to every person you meet, and it doesn't make you shy, uptight or ashamed of who you are. Talking about who you are can take up a lot of energy, and sometimes a way to save energy is to save certain information for people you love the most, and who love you back. If I'm walking down the street and someone asks me if there's a chemist's nearby, I can answer them with a few polite words, then move on. I don't have to offer them a guided tour of the whole town along with a detailed rundown of the events that've led to me being there that day. If I did that to everyone every time I went out, I'd be exhausted and so would they.

Who you decide to tell first will depend first of all on the people in your life and who is most important to you. Everyone's relationship with their family is different. Some people wait until their diagnosis is 'official' before talking to anyone; others find it helpful to talk to people as they research or wait for a diagnosis. Some people make a list of who they want to tell, while others decide more spontaneously. When you're deciding what to say it can help to ask yourself the following questions.

Have you given yourself some time to get used to your neurodivergence?

Having the urge to tell someone straight away is a good reason to believe that you're neurodivergent, and for others to believe and support you. But if it's something you first heard of a few days or a few moments ago, you might get a better response from others if you mention it once you've had time to learn about it and let it sit with you, especially if your moods and interests tend to come and go very quickly. This also especially goes for getting in touch with people from your past about it, which I'll say more about later on.

How much do you think this person knows about neurodivergence?

Although it's not always easy to assume, you can match what you say to what you think they might know. Unless someone introduces themselves as an expert, it's safest to assume they aren't one, although it's possibly fair to assume a neurotypical trainee nurse will know more than, say, a neurotypical second-hand car dealer. People are likely to have heard of ADHD, but what they know might not be accurate. They may have fewer misconceptions about dyspraxia, which can give you more room to explain.

How much have they told you or shared with you about themselves?

Someone who tells you everything about their life from how

much they hate their ex, to their ingrown toenail, is more likely to be comfortable finding out about you than someone you know little or nothing about.

Are you an Announcer or a Dropper?

Neurodivergence can be something you announce like a piece of life news, or you can drop it into the conversation in a more natural way, and there are pros and cons to both. In-person announcements are best for people who are close to you, people you know aren't busy, or if you're in a situation where you need formal support, like at work or at university.

'I've got something to tell you...' or 'Can we talk?' can sometimes make people feel anxious, and they might be prepared for something much worse, especially if you're also on edge, so try to reassure them.

A lot of people announce it on social media. If you feel up to doing this and you haven't already, it can be a good time for looking at your settings and who you're following, and checking you're happy with both.

You can also use the drop method to talk about things you're good at or struggle with without naming dyspraxia or ADHD, which can be helpful if you think people won't know what dyspraxia is, or will have stereotyped ideas, or if you're just not in the mood for a conversation. The downside is that being too casual can sometimes lead to people assuming you're joking.

Do you prefer to explain in your own way or someone else's?

Other people's online content or books (hint hint...) can be a super helpful way to explain neurodivergence, not to mention a super timesaver and a lovely hit of dopamine. Sharing funny videos, comics or infographics tends to go down well with most people, although if you're not sure it's best to ask before you post in group pages, and keep it to one or two, especially at work.

Do you need people to know without talking to them?
More about alert cards and disability lanyards in a moment...

Is it easier for you to explain in writing or in person?
This might be different for different people and in different situations. I always used to prefer to explain anything in writing as it gives me more time to organize my thoughts without going blank, rambling or constantly umm-ing and err-ing. And because, as I hope you can tell, I enjoy writing. But talking to someone in person means I can see and react to their reactions, and if I'm unsure how they'll react, I'm less likely to assume the worst, or get stuck in hyperfocus too long, which can often happen when I'm writing something that feels important. Keeping something in writing like an alert card or frequently asked questions list that you can give to others in person – again more of these in just a moment – can help with all these situations.

There's no such thing as the 'perfect' definition or explanation of neurodivergence, so be patient with yourself. As you get used to your diagnosis, you'll get more used to talking about it, and probably find you get more of an intuitive feel for how someone might react, and this can guide you in what to say and when. You'll also find you get more of an idea of which details you feel comfortable sharing. If you've already tried to talk to people and it hasn't gone as well as you'd expected, you'll find some hope in the next chapter.

'Should I tell someone else if I think they're neurodivergent?'

As I've mentioned already, recognizing that you're neurodivergent means you're likely to recognize traits in others.

Often the simplest way to find out whether someone is neurodivergent, or suggesting it to someone you think might be, is to mention your own. An ADHD friend of mine did this to a new colleague who'd confided in her about things she struggled with, and the colleague was very grateful.

Making direct and uninvited suggestions or observations is something to be more careful about. As a dyspraxic woman, I find that new people commenting that I look dyspraxic, however rightly or well-meaningly, can make me feel quite self-conscious or uncomfortable. Similarly, although sharing memes, links and self-discovery questionnaires can be fun, it might not be the best way to start a conversation with someone about their neurodivergence for the first time ever. Nor might printing out a diagnostic questionnaire and putting it in front of them unprompted (apologies to the person I once did this to), or tagging them on social media.

People sometimes ask me how to help someone who won't accept that they might be neurodivergent. It's never offensive to suggest someone is neurodivergent if it's done out of love and concern. But you can't force someone to accept a diagnosis, and trying to – especially if it's during an argument – will probably have the opposite effect.

Suggesting to someone that they might be neurodivergent could also make you feel very important to them. They may also feel very connected with you, especially if they feel lonely and unsupported. Lovely, if it's what you want. If you're not sure, this might not be something to bring up with them.

If you're a health or education professional and the person is someone in your care, then I'd argue it's part of your job to suggest it to them, whether or not you talk about your own neurodivergence at work. But not everyone agrees, and it's best to have the support of your manager or supervisor before you do this.

'Should I tell others about someone else's neurodivergence?'

If you're aware of someone else's neurodivergence, there are times it can be helpful to tell others about it so that they don't have to. Most obviously, this includes situations where they're less able to speak for themselves, like anxiety attacks, meltdowns or shutdowns.

Before group gatherings or events, I find it helpful if someone explains to everyone else that there are tasks I'd rather avoid because of my dyspraxia, or lets people we're visiting know that I need to have breakfast at a set time in the morning because of my ADHD medication.

If someone seems generally open and relaxed about their neurodivergence, they probably won't mind you mentioning it to people you both know in passing. But if it feels more as if someone is confiding in you about it and isn't used to talking about it, they might be more sensitive. If you're not sure, it's better to check with them first.

If you're talking about someone in a public performance, speech or book, you will need to make sure they can't recognize themselves, or get their permission to use their name or story.

It's kind to tell others about someone's neurodivergence to correct criticism or gossip, but try not to let the person know they're being criticized. I don't need to hear that your friend's third cousin thinks I fell over onto her husband deliberately...

> Chapter 6 has more about how to handle privacy when sharing your story, or someone else's.

'SO THIS IS ME! WHAT NOW?'

Alert cards, badges and lanyards

Pocket-sized alert cards or lanyards, like the sunflower lanyard scheme in the UK, are helpful for some neurodivergent people as they save time explaining and let people know you might need help or patience. I have mixed feelings about them. Sadly, being visibly disabled is far from a guarantee that strangers in the street will be more patient, helpful or kind to you. But if you find it hard to express yourself in stressful situations, having something quick and visual to hand can give you a feeling of backup.

If you forget or lose something and need a replacement or a refund, seeing that you have a lanyard or a card is more likely to make someone sympathetic, and to get pushback from others if they aren't. Once, during a heatwave, as I was about to board the train for the final leg of a seven-hour journey, I realized a blast from an air conditioning vent had blown the train ticket out of my pocket. The train guard took one look at me sweating, weeping and wearing a lanyard and simply waved me on with no bother.

You can buy a sunflower lanyard online for less than £5 (USD $6.25). Stickman Communications sells alert cards for dyspraxia and ADHD, as well as other neurodivergences, and a range of disabilities. Or you could design your own and choose the words that suit you. It doesn't have to be clinical and jargon-filled; I've seen people design witty pocket cards for questions or comments they're just tired of constantly hearing.

What to put on forms when you're asked about disability

Quite often, official forms ask questions about disability, such as 'Do you consider yourself to have a disability?' or 'Do you identify as disabled?'

There are two reasons you can be asked these questions:

1. So that you can be offered support, for example when you join a gym.
2. For equality and diversity monitoring. Publicly funded organizations have to collect certain statistics about who's using their services. This is to help them improve their services and make sure they're reaching the communities they serve.

It's up to you whether or how you choose to answer. I always tick the option for 'Neurodivergent', 'Dyspraxia' or 'ADHD' if they're there. If not, I go for 'Other' or 'Prefer not to say'. If there's just a Yes or No box, I might tick 'Yes', and if there's space, I will write in my diagnoses or put 'It depends on what you mean by a disability'.

Some tick-box forms use vaguer or broader definitions of disability like 'Cognitive', 'Sensory' or 'Learning disability'. These can mean different things to different people, so I don't tick them unless I'm sure what whoever's asking means by them.

Any form where you're asked the question should always make clear why you're being asked and who will see the response.

'Should I tell my employer, or potential employers, about my neurodivergence?'

Whether you tell your employer that you're neurodivergent depends on what kind of work you do, or are applying for, and how much the reasons for you finding out that you're neurodivergent are to do with work. If you're already working in a job that you enjoy, or if the job is just a stop-gap rather than a career, there might not seem much point, or it might not seem like a big deal. But work, or trying to balance work with everything else, is often why adults look for a diagnosis, and where we need the most understanding in order to be our best. As much as I would love this not to be the biggest, most frequently asked question about neurodivergent, I know all too well that having a good employer or manager can mean the difference between being able to work and not.

Dyspraxia, ADHD and the other neurodivergences are covered under the Equality Act in the UK, which means that they are treated as disabilities under the law and employers have to support you at work, just as they do employees with more visible disabilities. If you're looking for work, you can also ask for support at interview, or with your application. When I first applied for jobs back in the early-mid 2000s, mentioning a disability or asking for support before you'd been offered the job was often unheard of or frowned on, and this held me back a great deal.

If I had felt able to talk about neurodivergence at the application stage, or known what would help me, rather than worrying that I'd be seen as 'making a fuss', my early career could have looked very different. I wouldn't have failed interviews for jobs I would have been very good at, and ended up struggling in jobs I landed out of mutual desperation instead. Yes, some employers might have reacted badly. But the ones who'd been so disappointed and mystified that my interview hadn't lived up to the promise of my application might have been more understanding.

If you're applying for jobs, look for any information you can about diversity and inclusion wherever you apply. Although statements made on glossy company websites sadly don't always reflect reality, and how comfortable you're made to feel at work will depend a lot on who you work most closely with, it's a good sign if they at least have a statement, and an even better sign if they mention neurodivergence. If you're applying to an organization or a large business, the application form should ask whether you need any support or reasonable adjustments for your application, or at interview. You can use this space to mention anything that might help you, without having to be specific about your diagnosis or diagnoses if you don't feel ready to yet. If you're applying for a job in the UK, look out for something called the Guaranteed Interview scheme too. This means you're guaranteed an interview if you meet the requirements for the job, and it is meant to stop disabled people being discriminated against when looking for work. If you find job interviews difficult and if the feedback from interviewers says more about how you came across to them than your experience, mentioning your neurodivergence at the interview stage might be a good idea.

'Positive disclosures' or 'strengths-based disclosures' are becoming more popular in the workplace. I tend to prefer the words 'share' and 'tell' to 'disclose', which sounds both slightly stuffy and slightly seedy. But I'm using it here as I like the idea behind the word. A positive disclosure means mentioning neurodivergence as a way of selling yourself to an employer rather than just as a difficulty, and telling them about the things it makes you good at before you tell them about the things it makes harder for you. The strengths-based approach works best in firms that openly promote themselves as being inclusive and diverse or look for a particular skill associated with neurodivergence (and if it doesn't work, then they're not as inclusive or diverse as they say they are...).

For certain kinds of jobs, like those that involve driving or using machinery, you're required to tell your employer about certain disabilities or health conditions for health and safety reasons. This can include neurodivergence and almost certainly does if you take medication. It's understandable not to want to do this in case you're unfairly singled out as being a risk. But if you don't, you could face bigger problems later, especially if you're ever involved in an accident.

However and whenever you disclose (urgh, that word...), here are some basics:

Put something in writing, or another physical format that's easy to keep

Even if you work somewhere quite informal and feel okay talking to your colleagues face to face, it's usually a good idea to follow it up with something in writing. There are plenty of websites with articles and infographics you can share. Work and business coaches who work with neurodivergent people will also help you write something. Better still, design your own information.

Explain in a way that suits where you work, or want to work

The way you explain your neurodivergence to your new employer can be part of a strengths-based disclosure, giving you a chance to show off what you can do, and showing that you understand what they do. If you're a designer or good at visuals, design a great piece of content. If you work for a big corporate firm, present it as you would a report. If you work in a school, offer to give a presentation to staff or pupils. If you can find information about neurodivergent people doing well in your industry, show it to them. Look at the way they write to customers or service users and try to write or design something in that style. Writers and designers call this tone of voice and branding, and they're what help us connect with people we want to reach or get to know.

Let others know clearly about how 'out' you want to be at work

If you'd rather tell colleagues on a need-to-know basis, and you'd rather they heard it from you, make that clear to anyone you tell – especially if you're the exception in a company where lots of the staff live together or have known each other since school or university and drink together at weekends. But keeping too much information away from managers and relying on a few 'safe' colleagues might not be the sign of a healthy workplace.

If you're still not sure whether to tell

If you have any questions about your rights at work, the best thing to do is speak to your union if you have one, or look for advice from a local employment lawyer. Some law firms offer 'pro bono' (free) legal advice at local business centres, or, in the UK and Australia, Citizens Advice centres.

Final thoughts

Being open with anyone about your neurodivergence is, of course, a two-way thing. The next chapter is about other people's reactions or how they might react, and things to think about if understanding yourself better has made you want to get in touch with people from your past.

CHAPTER 4: A QUICK RECAP

- There's no right or wrong way to feel when you're learning about your neurodivergence – or perfect way to talk about it. How you feel about it is up to you. How you talk about it is something you'll develop over time.
- You don't owe everyone an explanation for your neurodivergence all the time. Wanting to explain it to everyone is very understandable. Choosing who you explain it to can save you energy.
- It's up to you whether you identify as disabled and whether you mention this on a form. But it can help people improve their service if you do.

CHAPTER 5

Other People's Reactions

The Best, the Worst and How to Handle Them

This chapter is about what might happen if you decide to tell people you're neurodivergent, or mention it in conversation. Like all of this book, it's based on my experience and those of hundreds of people I've met. I can't predict exactly how anyone specific in your life will react to knowing about your neurodivergence. Happily, I've had more good than bad reactions, and probably every neurodivergent person I know of has had a positive or helpful reaction from at least one other person they've spoken to about it. But if you've had a negative reaction, sadly, you're almost certainly not the only one either.

In the last chapter, I talked about who you might want to tell, when and why, so head back there if you missed it. Here, I've grouped some potential responses from best to worst to everything in-between. There's also a section on reconnecting with people from your past and whether to forgive someone who you feel has hurt you because of your neurodivergence…

The best reactions you can hope for

'Oh, great, me too!' Or being far more interested and clued-up than you expected
The first time I met another diagnosed dyspraxic person unintentionally and not at a dyspraxia event felt very rare and special. These days, thanks to many more people being diagnosed, it's far more likely for you than it was for me in my twenties for ADHD or dyspraxia to find this out about someone in casual conversation at work, online or out and about than at a support group or conference.

'Thanks for telling me, I'm glad you felt you could' and 'Let me know if there's anything I can do to help'
These reactions are great because they show that someone is listening, keeping the focus on you, and letting you lead the conversation.

Saying sorry for upsetting you, or not doing more to help
People you're close to might feel that they should have known or done more. Sometimes this can feel very healing and sometimes it can feel more difficult. There's more about deciding whether to forgive someone who's hurt you because of your neurodivergence later in this chapter.

Other common reactions

'I think I (or someone else) might be'
This happens more often than you think. Sometimes it can be fun; like the feeling when you tell someone about somewhere really exciting you've just been and they sound dead keen to check it out. Other times, it can feel more like being the IT person

or plumber who always gets asked to fix tech problems or leaky taps whenever they go to other people's houses. It's up to you how you answer depending on where you are and how you feel. If someone directly asks you for examples of neurodivergent traits you've noticed in them, you can be honest. If not, it's better to avoid being too specific, as it can make them feel self-conscious or embarrassed. Even if they're a really good friend and you can rattle off ten examples of times they've fallen over in public or lost their keys, they might not be ready to hear it from you yet.

'My friend/sister has that'
Statistically, almost everyone knows someone who's neurodivergent, so you'll hear this one a lot. Most often, people say this in passing as a way of relating to you or making you feel comfortable. Other times, the person may really want to talk about it, and go on to ask for advice about whoever it is. An uncomfortable variation is: 'My son has that/is disabled, but not like you! He's really disabled!' My friend's reply to this is: 'My Aunty Sue's neurotypical, but not like you!'

'Yeah, I thought so!', 'Is that why you...?'
Depending on who it is, having confirmation that someone knew before you did can feel like a comfort and a relief, or it might feel a bit intrusive and make you self-conscious, especially if they bring up something very specific that you've done or said.

And common questions

'You mean dyslexia?'
The best way to avoid this one is to explain what dyspraxia is as soon as you use the word. If you've clearly explained the difference and they still think you're dyslexic, they either have attention problems or don't really care.

'Have you tried...?'
If you have experience of other disabilities, you probably don't need me to tell you how annoying this one can be.

'Is it caused by...?'
'No one's really sure' is the quickest answer. If you were born early, you can say this is the most likely cause. If it doesn't matter to you, you can say that too.

'Is there a cure?', 'Would you want one if there was?'
How you answer this one is up to you. My own thoughts are in Chapter 1.

The worst reactions

Pitying you or being scared for you as soon as you mention anything
As a society, we still often treat any mention of disability as something to be pitied or feared and we feel uncomfortable talking about it. None of this is your fault and you don't have to apologize for how information about you makes anyone else feel. The best thing to say is simply, 'You don't have to feel sorry for me.'

Some people fear the worst if they hear an unfamiliar medical-sounding word, especially if English isn't their first language. I've had to reassure distraught people that dyspraxia won't directly kill them or their child.

Immediately switching to talking to you as if you're five years old
I have rarely, if ever, had this reaction, but sadly know people who have. It's most common from teachers and other professionals who work with children and don't realize neurodivergent

adults exist. You can just say calmly, 'I know you work with children, but I'm grown-up and I can understand you. You can talk to me in your normal voice.'

'What does that mean?', 'Whoah, slow down!'
This isn't necessarily a bad reaction but it can make you feel cut off, especially if someone interrupts straight away and sound dismissive. People who react like this often do it because they feel threatened or put off by a word they don't understand, or by you talking super-fast, which you might be if you're keen.

'But everyone does that!'
My two favourite responses are 'Everyone wees, but if you wee 30 times a day, and don't know why, you're probably not very happy' and 'We all have blood pressure, but some people's is higher or lower than others'.

Not taking you seriously
If you're dyspraxic, you probably know the sinking feeling that can come with being asked to help set up at a busy in-person event where you hardly know anyone. Parties, group holidays, fundraisers or conferences can suddenly end up being a tangle of unfamiliar venues, people, outfits and equipment. My go-to at these is to announce with a smile that I'm the least dexterous person ever in an attempt to casually break the ice, and then try my best to do whatever I'm being asked to. The downside of this is that sometimes people treat it as a joke, false modesty, or worse, a weak attempt to try and avoid doing something boring. If this happens, I try to shrug it off temporarily and explain more fully in a quiet moment, when people tend to be very apologetic. But if you're not in the mood to laugh at yourself or correct misunderstandings, it's okay to avoid casual mentions and wait for situations where you have time and space for the fuller explanation.

'So what?', 'Who cares?'

This sort of reaction can come from innocently trying to get to know someone who's not interested in talking to you or listening to you and thinks kindness is beneath them. I once heard it from someone who aspired to do a job which might have involved interviewing bereaved parents, and I can only hope they never had to. If you're feeling brave, you could try a salty comeback, 'Oh, I'm so sorry for boring you!', or: 'Well, as it happens, I don't find your loud chat about [whatever] thrilling either, but I'm a nicer person than you and don't say so.' Otherwise, you can safely assume they're not worth a minute of your time.

Throwing out myths and stereotypes

This can be done in a hostile way ('Oh, you won't be able to sit still then?') or with good intentions ('You must be very high functioning!'). Either way, it can be extremely annoying. If you feel up to challenging, you could practise some replies to common myths and misunderstandings. The information in Chapters 1 and 2 will help you with this. Or just say 'That's actually a myth' or 'That's not true for everyone'. Sometimes the way to avoid myths is to describe yourself and what you need rather than use the label: 'I find it hard to concentrate when I'm sitting by the window!' But if they get more dismissive ('Oh, I find it hard to focus', 'Don't we all!'), you might have to be more direct, if you think it's worth it.

Saying that your neurodivergence is God's gift or punishment

I personally prefer not to involve the big G in any discussion about my brain, and expect anyone in my life to respect that. You have every right to expect the same.

Criticizing you for using tech that helps you

Thankfully, most technology that makes life easier for neurodivergent people is also a big part of modern life for most people.

If you're unfortunate enough to meet a rare bore who makes hating sat navs or phone apps a part of their personality, just repeat that yes, you do need whatever it is in a suitably firm voice until they give up.

Well-meant but tricky compliments

- 'But you're young/clever/pretty/funny! You should be happy!'
- 'You're so brave!'
- 'I don't see you as being disabled.'
- 'I'd never have guessed!' Okay if it's from my spin class instructor; worse if it's from a colleague followed by: 'I just thought you were a bit weird/awkward/ditzy.'

People I've heard these from include people who've gone on to be diagnosed with types of neurodivergence themselves (and are lovely).

If you struggle to react to questions...

Lots of neurodivergent people find it difficult to answer big questions or deal with reactions on the spot. If someone asks a question which is difficult for you to answer straight away, or reacts in a difficult way, try the following:

- **Count to three in your head and start again:** Especially if you're nervous and finding it difficult to find the right words, or if someone's clearly not taking in what you're saying. If you talk very fast and people say they find it hard to understand you, another tip I learned from a drama student is to say the words 'full stop' to yourself in your head at the end of sentences.

- **Offer to talk more another time or message someone instead of talking in person:** You're in a bar and you get talking to someone who seems interested but suddenly you're tired, or you're in a group and a noisy stag do walks in and suddenly it's not so fun anymore. Sound familiar? Sometimes it's easiest to leave a conversation for later than struggle on.

- **Say 'Actually, hold on...' and come up with an excuse to leave:** This is best for people who are just annoying or plain uncomfortable and who you want as little to do with as possible.

If it's difficult to tell how the conversation is going...

When you're talking to someone about something you're super interested in, it can be hard to read or take in how they're feeling and reacting, even if it's something you find easy at other times. Sometimes not being able to tell how someone feels can be more uncomfortable than if it's blatantly obvious either way. If you're talking about neurodivergence and you're not sure how someone feels, or whether someone's as interested as you are, you could try saying:

- 'How does it make you feel to know?'
- 'Would you like me to say more?'
- 'I only found out about this quite recently, and I'm really into it, as you can probably tell...!'

- 'Shall we talk about something else? How are you?'

That way, you're acknowledging the other person's feelings without apologizing for yours. Their reaction will help you decide where to take the conversation from there. If they say 'Oh please carry on, this stuff's really interesting!', you can. And if they'd rather talk about something else, they can change the subject. This goes for anything you might be really interested in.

Another common reaction is that someone you tell says little or nothing. The most likely reasons for this are that they're busy, not sure what to say or simply not surprised. When I announced my ADHD diagnosis on social media, most of my followers said nothing at all. I took that to mean I might as well have posted that water was wet.

If someone you really care about reacts badly...

From outright disbelief (which is thankfully less common than it used to be) to not understanding (which is sadly still more common), someone important to you reacting badly to your diagnosis can be deeply hurtful. There are a few reasons why people you love or want to impress most can react in the worst way.

You caught them at a bad time
People are more likely to react negatively to important information when they're stressed or busy. As above, this can be worked through if they're willing to apologize.

They react critically to things they don't understand
Most people do this from time to time, and up to a point it can be healthy. If they're willing to accept when it might come across as hurtful or dismissive and apologize, this is usually resolvable.

They feel guilty or ashamed
People you love probably want to feel that they've done their best for you and that they make you happy and may resent your diagnosis because they see it as making them look bad. They may recognize themselves in you but not be ready to admit it, or resent you looking for support they've never had.

You've masked well
Although disbelief may be more common from people you don't know well because they're easiest to mask in front of, you're just as likely to have tried to hide your challenges from people you love, especially as you get older. At school, where I had to do lots of things I didn't want to with lots of people I didn't want to be around, it was more obvious to people that I was different, even if they couldn't pinpoint how or why. By my twenties, I was spending most of my time writing or socializing with people in short bursts, mainly at sit-down venues where clumsiness and an inability to understand numbers or pay attention to the right things were less obvious.

To some of those I knew best at the time, I wasn't a neurodivergent woman struggling to live up to people's expectations in a neurotypical world, I was an insecure drama queen always worrying about nothing, who had every reason to be happy if only I chose to be. Rather than seeing dyspraxia as the reason for my problems, they saw it as a real but basically fairly insignificant illness I was suddenly blaming all my problems on due to being an insecure drama queen. And I still only had half a diagnosis! My unsupported neurodivergence was, in fact, even more to blame for my problems than I or anybody knew at the time.

They blame all your difficulties on your background
Coming from a background that's either underprivileged or privileged can make neurodivergence harder for those around you

to see and accept. If you had a difficult upbringing, people might prefer to blame trauma for all your difficulties rather than accept that neurodivergence has also played a part, or just be too immersed in their own problems to worry about yours. Some people's negative reactions can also be related to stigma around medication, which there's more on in Chapter 8.

They're not someone you can happily be close to

Having a different neurotype to someone else is like any other difference. It can make you incompatible with someone, or point to other things that make you incompatible. Whatever their reasons, anyone who doesn't accept your neurodivergence is denying something very important about you. And while an imperfect reaction isn't automatically a reason to cut someone out of your life, no one deserves to have you fixate forever on trying to make them understand you. Intensity and 'overthinking' often go with being neurodivergent and can make life challenging. They're also a very usual part of being a young woman, and I let older men make me feel as if they were inherently bad things which indicated that I was flawed and broken. Don't do the same.

If this person is someone you can't avoid, or depend on

Of course, sadly, it might not be possible or practical to avoid someone as much as you'd like to. Support from a professional or peer support networks may be able to help you reduce or limit the time you spend with them or the support you need from them. There's more about this later in the book.

> For more on this topic, see 'Should I forgive someone who's hurt me because of my neurodivergence?' later in this chapter.

If you feel someone's reaction discriminates against you...

The most negative ways someone can react to your neurodivergence fall under abuse, discrimination or both. Examples of abuse are physical or sexual assault, hate speech, threats or controlling behaviour. Discrimination specifically applies to behaviour in organizations and institutions, like employers, businesses or service providers. There are two types:

1. **Direct discrimination** is when someone treats you unfavourably because of a disability or other protected characteristic; for example, if you mention neurodivergence to someone and they make dismissive or derogatory remarks or suddenly start to exclude you from doing things you've been doing fine because they assume your neurodivergence makes you less able.

2. **Indirect discrimination** is when an organization's policies or practices unintentionally or unknowingly put you at a disadvantage compared to others because of a disability. This covers not just how people react to your neurodivergence but is about how everything in the world works for or against you because of who you are.

Dyspraxic people or ADHDers are often indirectly discriminated against when bad design or bad practice leaves us more open to mistakes. For example, if you miss important appointments or instructions because you don't get sent automatic reminders, or someone only communicates with you one way. Or if a form or piece of software doesn't have a built-in spellcheck to pick up typos or audio-visual cues to stop you entering the wrong information by mistake. Not being allowed to use your phone or headphones in a space can also be indirectly discriminatory if you need them to support you.

When you're talking about being discriminated against, directly or indirectly, it can feel easier to downplay what's happened, or hide your feelings behind others rather than call it what it is. Sadly, this makes it harder for people to understand or help you. In my early twenties, not long after my dyspraxia diagnosis, I had an interview for a training course with someone who reacted negatively when I mentioned it. But rather than emphasizing that detail to people when I vented about it afterwards, often I just told them she was a horrible woman, who probably taught people how to do the job because she'd failed at it herself. Someone frostily pointed out to me that women tend to leave their jobs to teach because it fits better around looking after children or ageing parents.

You're more likely to get others on your side if you explain specifically what's happened to you and why it's wrong. For example, 'When I told Jane about my dyspraxia, she scoffed at me and rolled her eyes' or 'Being judged on my handwriting when I wouldn't need to write by hand in a real situation means I'm excluded for being dyspraxic' instead of 'Jane was a complete cow to me from the minute I walked into the room' or 'Handwritten tests are so unfair! Who even uses a pen anymore?!'

As my example shows, it's also best to vent to the safest people about discrimination first, and talk to others when you feel calmer.

There is an ever-increasing number of ways to speak out against discrimination, and, happily, increasing numbers of organizations open to learning and doing better.

Here are some pointers for certain situations.

Applying for jobs and courses

Most unfair recruitment practices happen because of a lack of understanding about neurodivergence, and disability generally. If you've applied for a job or course and feel you've been disadvantaged by something an employer or organization did or didn't do during an interview or application process, it's worth letting them know. You can learn a lot from their reaction, and as long as you don't burn the place down and swear at them, a good employer will see you as proactive and thoughtful. If a place has treated you so badly you want nothing more to do with them for life, it's also worth letting them know. It might make you feel better, and hopefully even change things for applicants in the future.

> See 'Should I tell my employer, or potential employers, about my neurodivergence?' in Chapter 4 for more on talking about neurodivergence at work.

In healthcare

Lots of health professionals are brilliant at their jobs, including many who are themselves neurodivergent. Sadly, there are also some so-called 'caring' professionals who in my opinion treat neurodivergent and disabled people appallingly. There is still a very big gap between medical and social understandings of disability as they apply to neurodivergence too. If you feel that you need to complain about a specific healthcare person, you can write to their professional association, such as the General Medical Council (GMC) in the UK, or your state's Medical Board in the US. Some doctors publish their GMC number online. If you're in England, your healthcare provider should have something called Patient Advice and Liaison Service (PALS).

I wrote to mine when a professional at my then-local hospital kindly told me I was too old to have anxiety attacks that were caused by my rampant grief and untreated ADHD. Unfortunately, I couldn't remember their name or many identifying details because of (you've guessed it) anxiety and, luckily, I had enough good, helpful people in my life not to believe their opinion of me or my brain. But I wish I had taken my complaint further, and dread to think what a young girl would have felt if she'd gone to the doctor about her mental health for the first time.

More recently, I've complained about stigma related to ADHD medication. There's more about this in Chapter 8.

Businesses and services

For any kind of business, the best person to speak or write to is usually the manager or supervisor. If the person who's been unkind or thoughtless is the manager, see if there's a regional or head office. If there's somewhere you can leave a negative review, this often has an impact and can make sure other customers don't have the same experience.

Where else to find help with abuse or discrimination

If none of the above resolves the situation, a disability rights organization may be able to help. Details of UK and worldwide support organizations are given at the end of this book.

If you feel you can't complain, or let go after an incident

One of the cruellest things about neurodivergence is it can make doing things harder and make you dwell on things you didn't do, including standing up for yourself! If you're worried it's 'too late' to say anything, you might be able to say your neurodivergence was part of why you delayed getting in touch (after all, it's true!).

If your diagnosis is making you feel bad about an incident that happened a very long time ago and you've never told anyone about it, is there a safe way you could do it now?

Ultimately, you and those who know your situation well are

the best people to decide if and when complaining is worth your energy or will change anything. Not complaining or going public about being badly treated for any reason doesn't make you any more to blame for what happened.

Dealing with past relationships

'Should I get back in touch with someone from my past and explain my neurodivergence?'

When you're going back over your life after a diagnosis, it's very common to want to explain it to people who didn't understand you when you were younger. Whether or not this is helpful depends on why you're getting in touch. Before you do, it's good to be as clear as you can in your mind about what you want to happen from it. If they very clearly ended whatever relationship you had and you're hoping that writing and explaining everything will change their mind and turn you into their new bestie – or if you ended things with them and now want to try again – you're more likely to be disappointed.

It's also really common to wonder whether the reason you lost touch with someone or hear from them much less has something to do with your neurodivergence and want to write to them and say sorry when there's actually no reason to. In my experience, pouring your heart into a written apology and inviting someone onto a call or for a meetup, then getting back a quick couple of lines of reassurance, can feel almost as crappy as never knowing whether you've upset someone at all.

Although you might have the urge to write pages and pages going over an event or telling them about everything you've been doing since you saw them, this is one situation where 'less is more' probably applies. Keeping it down to 400–500 words at most is probably comfortable. (And even that will seem like a lot to some recipients!) If like me and many neurodivergent people you have an exceptionally good long-term memory, it's best to assume the person you're writing to doesn't remember things as clearly as you do. Unless you know for a fact that something you did hurt them deeply, it's likely they haven't thought about it as much as you have.

It's also a good idea to give yourself at least a few months to get used to a diagnosis before you get in touch with people from your past, and not do it at a time when you're stressed or busy, even though this may be when it feels most urgent. It's very difficult to see this when you're fixated, as it's very difficult to see beyond the now. But from experience, the more burningly I've felt the urge to get in touch with someone *right now* and that if I didn't I'd regret it *forever*, the more I've realized later on that it would have been better to wait. Even if you're literally about to emigrate and it feels as if you'll never get another chance to see them again, I promise you will. And whether it's in another year or in five years' time, it'll be better than putting pressure on yourself right now. If you feel you've put off getting in touch and it's led to things being left unresolved, you could ask someone you trust to help you come up with a better plan and hold you accountable for sticking to it. There's more about accountability in the next chapter.

A popular way to deal with unresolved past feelings is to write a letter to someone and keep it for yourself without sending it. This is a good idea if writing to someone directly would put you in danger or cause more problems for you than it would solve. The problem with unsent letters is that if you enjoy writing they can trap you in hyperfocus rather than helping you move on with your life. If you've been writing and tinkering with one for weeks or months, ask yourself (and ideally a trusted other person) what's the worst that could happen if you just hit send and either do it, or delete it.

Often the main reason for wanting to get in touch with someone from many years ago is to let them know you've changed and grown. Most people change, grow and learn to see things differently as they get older, and anyone who knew you as a child or a teenager will assume you have without needing to meet up with you in person to prove it. Probably the most realistic way to get in touch with someone is to let them know you aren't expecting more than a quick acknowledgement. If you're messaging or emailing someone, you could even include a link to a one-click form so that they can let you know they've seen your message easily and fast without having to write back to you directly.

'Should I forgive someone who's hurt me because of my neurodivergence?'

There are three kinds of people who've hurt me at some time in my life:

1. People at school who were mean because they were generally mean and didn't really like anyone ever. I hope some of them have grown into nicer people; some probably haven't changed, but basically, I never have to see them again and don't really care.

2. People who I now understand didn't like me because they had their own 'stuff' going on and my strengths and weaknesses both seemed like a threat to them. It's a cliché that the worst bullies are unhappy themselves and that some situations have no winners, but it is one I've known to be profoundly true. While I was putting together this book, I found out that someone who I experienced as having bullied me had died suddenly and tragically. I don't wish this on anybody.

3. Well-meaning people who've hurt me by not understanding me very well. If I couldn't forgive people in this category, there would probably be nobody left in my life. Things that are now regarded as unhelpful and possibly abusive things to do to a distressed child or young person (yelling in their face to make them listen or stop talking, mocking their tone of voice or appearance or threatening to record them and play it back to make them calm down, and calling their anxiety selfish) were also pretty common and accepted when I was growing up.

Therapy has helped me understand many of these situations or the relationships behind them, and hold lots of different feelings in my head at the same time. ADHD medication helps me the most in stopping unwanted past memories popping up constantly when I don't want them.

I can't tell you for sure whether you should forgive someone or not. Forgiveness is a complicated, personal thing that rarely happens in one go or overnight. I can tell you that you deserve people in your life who make you feel good and to spend less time around people who consistently make you feel bad. These questions can help you if you're struggling with how to keep someone who's hurt you in your life:

- **What does forgiveness mean to you or this person?** Forgiving someone isn't the same as forgetting how someone made you feel or thinking it doesn't matter. To me – and to pretty well every neurodivergent woman I speak to about their lives – it often means being able to hold a lot of different feelings in my head at the same time. There's more on this in the next chapter.

- **What positives does this person add to your life?** This isn't necessarily answered by their relationship to you. No one has an automatic right to forgiveness just because of who they are or how long you've known them.

- **Will forgiveness help you heal or open you up to more harm?** If you keep being hurt in the same way, the more important question is not to forgive someone but how to stop being hurt.

Final thoughts

This chapter is about people's reactions to your neurodivergence. There's more about relationships in general in Chapter 11.

The most positive or negative reactions aren't always immediate and both negative and positive attitudes can reveal themselves over time. If you've experienced discrimination or abuse at any time, or you aren't sure, once again, please look for qualified information and support. There are some helpful organizations mentioned at the end of the book.

It's understandable that negative reactions tend to stick most in our memories. I'd love to hear from readers who've had positive reactions.

The next chapter is about sharing your experiences with a wider audience.

CHAPTER 5: A QUICK RECAP

- Expect some 'me too' reactions to your neurodivergence. It's likely you know other neurodivergent people who haven't told you or don't know they are. The more people

you talk about your neurodivergence, the more other neurodivergent people you're likely to come across.
- Not everyone will react perfectly to your neurodivergence straight away. But you deserve people in your life who want to understand. Others may need some time and space to understand your neurodivergence, or to accept that they might be neurodivergent too. That doesn't mean you should put all your energy into winning someone else's approval or acceptance.
- Connecting with other neurodivergent people may be helpful if you don't get the reaction you'd like from people you know. There's more about this in the next couple of chapters.

CHAPTER 6

Sharing Your Story with the World

So far, this book has been about recognizing neurodivergence and talking to people in your life about it. This chapter is about sharing your experiences with a wider audience. Lots of neurodivergent people share their experiences to practise their skills as designers, writers or coders, make a bit of money during a dry spell, or as part of working through their feelings.

For me, being publicly dyspraxic has been both a way of meeting other neurodivergent people and an easy way to bring it up with people in my life when they asked what I was working on ('I'm doing a talk about dyspraxia'). It's also helped people recognize dyspraxia – and since my more recent diagnosis, ADHD – in themselves. In this chapter, I'm sharing what I've learned about sharing, from my own experiences and my observations of others.

Of course, not all neurodivergent people can or want to talk publicly about being neurodivergent. Some people can't easily do so because their jobs involve national security or something similar. Some people may find it harder than others to do so because of accompanying disabilities or health needs. Others don't feel the need to talk about it, or even see themselves as neurodivergent; often because they work or spend time in spaces where neurodivergent traits are seen as ordinary, like tech, engineering, architecture or certain fan communities. But the reason I choose to is exactly that: to make it more normal everywhere.

Sharing your experience is sometimes called 'lived experience' work. Having 'lived experience' of something means having personal experience of it. This can apply to any experience but tends to mean being from a minoritized community.

Ways to share your experiences

The main ways you can share your experience around being neurodivergent are by creating your own online content, appearing in the media, giving talks and workshops, taking part in research or consultancy, or posting and commenting on online communities. I'll go through each one here.

Creating your own online content

Until very recently, if you had something to say or a story to tell, you had to talk to a newspaper or be on TV. Now, as a neurodivergent person, you're most likely to create your own content on social media platforms, which gives you much more control over what you post than traditional media. You're likely to have come across popular neurodivergent content creators across TikTok, X (formerly Twitter), Instagram and Substack. Many of these are geared towards ADHD and autism. There are also some dyspraxic content creators like Tumi (aka The Black Dyspraxic) and the Dyspraxia Collective, which was set up to be an online hub for the dyspraxia community after the closure of the Dyspraxia Foundation in 2024.

This section isn't about how to become an influencer with a superstar following, because I don't think I am one, I don't think that should be anyone's aim and I don't think most people actually start out wanting to be that even if they end up with a big following. However, having been writing for online audiences in different ways for 20 years, I know a thing or two about how to have a good experience online.

Like any relationship with anything, the key to being happy making content is to try to check in with yourself about what kind of a relationship you have and want with the platform you're using. Because a lot of people don't set out to become big creators, they also don't think about why they're posting content or which platform is best for what message they want to communicate. For instance, lots of neurodivergent aspiring writers and bloggers now use X and Instagram as writing tools or for general brain dumps. But these platforms were designed for short messages, and long and detailed posts several times a day can feel quite exhausting for followers, especially ADHDers and dyspraxics who might prefer not to constantly scroll through a tonne of text or type into a tiny box. Platforms like Substack which are designed for writers and bloggers are often, in my view, better ways to practise writing. To put it more bluntly, if you're posting on X more than a few times a day, you could think about working on a different platform.

Similarly, trying to fit complex messages into short videos may mean the message gets lost or loses meaning – there's more on this in the section on online communities later in this chapter.

Sharing your story anywhere public can lead to other people responding in ways that are difficult or triggering for you, and this is especially true online and on social media. I always signpost people to relevant support organizations that are run by trained counsellors.

The more followers your content has, the more of your time it can take up. An editor I used to know reckoned that after 10,000 followers, it becomes literally impossible for anyone to run their own account. I'd say it's half that number, and even a jump from a handful of followers to a few hundred can feel immense. When I had my first social media accounts, there were very few ways to get help managing a large following. Now, as well as more options built into apps to control replies, there are hundreds of social media agencies that do this. Don't be afraid to use them if you need to. In the UK, if you're self-employed and in a new business or your turnover is above a certain amount, you may qualify for an assistant through Access to Work.

If your diagnosis is very new, especially if you don't have experience of running a social media channel with a lot of followers, it's a good idea to start creating for friends or a small number of followers at first, and 'try out' your content on a locked or restricted account.

Appearing in the media, like newspapers or on TV

Here I'm including being interviewed for articles or on TV, as well as writing articles based around your own opinions or experiences, sometimes called 'comment pieces' or 'first person pieces'.

As a former journalist, I believe there are two things that separate responsible journalism from the irresponsible journalism that gives the rest a bad name. Responsible journalists care about whether sharing their story will be good for them and for their reputation in the long term, not just whether it'll help them in the short term. I'm very grateful for the places I've told my story over the years, and just as grateful for the places where I haven't. Some articles I wrote or pitched as a young journalist when I needed money quickly either weren't published or were significantly changed because the editor felt they would cause problems for me or the publication. A responsible editor, manager or organization should take the time to find out about you before you share your story, and should ask and listen to what you need to make it easier.

Responsible journalists also care that your story is yours and won't just change it to fit whichever one they want to tell. They also don't pressure you into anything you don't want to do, or withhold information from you that would influence your decision to appear in an article or programme.

If you're thinking of appearing in the press or on TV, you can use the list below to help you.

A checklist of things to find out before you appear in the media or in public

Where will your story appear?
The most important thing to remember is the first line of every internet safety lesson: anything that's published online tends to stay there for a long time. Are you happy with your story being at the top of search results for your name for years, or even decades? (Obviously, neurodivergent people are likely to Google you...)

Will you have any control over where it's shared or who by?
Unless you're talking to a selected audience who've had to hand in their phones beforehand, the answer is almost always no.

Are others mentioned in your story?
See 'Privacy issues around story sharing' later in the chapter for more on this.

Are you appearing with others, and if so, who?
You might be asked to record or film with other people. You should be told this and are entitled to ask who else will be appearing.

Does the content maker or event organizer have lived experience?
If they have, they're far more likely to represent you in a way you're happy with.

What message does this piece or event want to get across with your story?
It's important that you know and are happy with why an organization wants to tell your story, otherwise the very worst places will just use your name and change whatever you say to fit in with whatever they want, or whatever they decide they want later. I don't share my story somewhere if they want something that's overly positive or negative and the truth of my situation doesn't fit with either. If they aren't sure about what they want when they approach me, I encourage them to come back when they are.

How do they headline and promote their content?
Even if you have full say over the content of your story, you probably won't get to decide how it looks on the page or gets shared on social media, and seeing it reduced to a clickbait-y headline can be a shock. (The first article I ever wrote about dyspraxia for a national paper was headlined: *'I'm dyspraxic, not useless...'*)

Is there a consent form?
You should be asked for your written consent to be filmed,

or for video of you to be shared online. If you get given anything to sign, read it before you do, or ask someone else to check it over if it's long and wordy.

Speaking at events or delivering training

Charities and professional organizations trying to improve services for neurodivergent people often invite neurodivergent people to give talks and workshops about our experiences. Although most probably won't attract as big an audience, as with appearing in the media, the more you know before the event the better. These are some questions I look for answers to when I'm asked to speak at an event or deliver training.

First, is the event for or about neurodivergent people? In recent years, organizations have got much better at letting neurodivergent people lead events about our lives rather than asking us to listen to professionals talking about us. But if an event is aimed at professional audiences, you might want to do some research into how many attendees have lived experience as well as, or alongside, their professional experience. It's a good sign if other speakers, workshop leaders or delegates are people who seem open about their neurodivergence online.

If you're being asked to talk about the workplace, what is the host organization doing or intending to do to make life better for their neurodivergent employees? And do they employ people to do *your* job, or a job you're aspiring to? I'm asked to do talks by law firms and banks even though most of my experience is in the media and the charity sector. I don't mind, but organizations I can actually see myself fitting into tend to get more out of me.

Then there are practical questions, including things like who the audience is and who you're appearing with, and the timings of the day. It's also helpful to ask how you will be introduced when your 'bit' starts. It can throw me off when the introduction repeats my own introduction, so I have to repeat myself or think of something else to say.

For in-person events, I find out whether there's food or drink available at the venue so I can plan accordingly. If there is, I also ask whether there's somewhere to sit down so I don't have to decorate my chest with a buffet. It's also helpful to let people know what your preferences are when it comes to physical contact; for example, whether or not you like to hug or shake hands as a greeting.

For online events where I'm presenting, I always ask for this to be pre-recorded, or at the very least, for a run through of the tech before the day. I sometimes do Q&As, but it's okay to ask people to submit questions in advance if you prefer.

Live talks and broadcast media appearances sometimes involve processing different sorts of information at once, like listening to a live feed of questions while being given instructions from a producer or manager. This is a nightmare for many neurodivergent people and you're right to request not to have to do it.

The timing of an event can also be an important decider. It's easy to underestimate the amount of work involved in an event and take on too many. I always budget for at least half a day of preparation time, or more if it's a longer event.

Several neurodivergent speakers I know have been asked to do talks about neurodivergence at work for organizations immediately after they've applied for and been rejected for a job. It's up to you whether you think this is valuable or whether it feels like an insulting consolation prize.

Taking part in research, or being a consultant

There's more to sharing your story than just standing in front of an audience. Another way of using your experiences to improve things for other neurodivergent people is by taking part in research and consultancy. By 'research' I mean academic or medical research. I'm using 'consultancy' as an umbrella term for any type of experience sharing that doesn't fit into any of the other categories.

There's still far too little academic research into adult neurodivergence, especially into ADHD and dyspraxia specifically. Thankfully, this is beginning to change. I've taken part in studies about dyspraxic adults' experiences of exercise and into the effect of ADHD on emotional wellbeing, for example, and these sorts of opportunities regularly appear on mailing lists, on social media and in online communities.

While media work is often one-off or short term, reactive and fast paced, research and consultancy are more inclined to be the opposite. Unlike the scattergun approach of some journalists, academic researchers tend to have very specific and upfront requirements for whom they want to speak to and why. You should always be asked to sign a consent form which clearly sets out the purpose of the research, where your answers will be stored and for how long, and your right to withdraw from the research at any time.

Consultancy can be a one-off experience like a focus group, or it can involve ongoing work for an organization. Some charities and organizations run organized networks or a pool of consultants where you regularly take part in opportunities as and when they come along. This is sometimes called 'lived experience work'. The term 'lived experience' means someone with experience. I'm part of a brilliantly organized lived experience network run by a mental health charity where I use my experience of neurodivergence to promote good mental health and provide support on a freelance basis to the communications team.

Getting paid to share your experiences

Quite simply, sharing your experience in any form involves work, and work deserves to be paid. Budgets vary and what's offered may also depend on your experience, but as a guide, if you're in the UK, an hourly rate equivalent to the national minimum wage is the minimum you should accept. Average freelance rates for content creators like copywriters and designers range from £250 to £450 a day (or approximately USD $300–550).

You might not always get paid if you're appearing in someone else's work, like being interviewed for a podcast, livestream or on TV or radio, but they should either let you take part remotely or cover any expenses, such as travel and accommodation.

For any opportunity, but especially where there's money or expenses involved, you should get written confirmation of what you're being paid and what you're being asked to do.

Despite what the occasional media article might say, being a neurodivergence or disability consultant is unlikely to be your path to fame and fortune. But it is possible to make a living, or a significant chunk of your income, from it if you want to. This starts with knowing your worth, which can be difficult if you're a neurodivergent person who's had less-than-positive experiences at work.

Some organizations that support neurodivergent people (especially small charities) have unfortunately tended to benefit from our lack of self-worth by getting a lot of free work out of us. Others don't necessarily mean to take the mickey, but tend to attract disabled volunteers or low-paid workers by giving them the impression they're doing something that's a full-time job or likely to lead to one. When you're desperate for money, it's easy to take whatever you can get, or to get carried away with excitement and assume someone wants to pay you because you need them to. It's not pushy to ask people about money, it's sensible.

Posting and commenting in online communities

There are now many online communities like Reddit as well as social media platforms where large numbers of neurodivergent people gather. There are many ways and reasons this is a good thing and ways it can be challenging.

The online neurodivergent community is great above all because it's accessible and highlights the importance of us being heard. Those ADHD memes are easy to carry around and share. They're often funny and relatable. They reach people who don't have a diagnosis, who aren't interested in going to conferences or who can't get to support groups. And they give us spaces to talk about ourselves and among ourselves, rather than endlessly hearing other people talk over us about what it's like to live with us. We can talk or write about our neurodivergence online as much as we like, and post cat photos from the same account if we want to.

Why online communities can get tricky is because there often isn't space to explain things fully and answer big questions in a nuanced way. Add in that they're made up of many different people who are at different stages of understanding themselves and their neurodivergence and have had some amount of difficulty in their lives, and it is obvious how easily arguments can start, and misinformation can spread. Neurodivergent people often notice and label relatable physical symptoms as being part of neurodivergence without understanding or explaining why they are. Then we post about it online, leading to sneers of: 'Oh, people on the internet are saying being thirsty and having dark circles under your eyes are a neurodivergent thing now!'

The same goes for behaviour. For example, a claim which has spread through online communities is that reacting to someone's funny story by telling one about yourself is part of neurodivergence. I don't think it is, and actually, most people do it all the time whether they're neurodivergent or not. But it can look as if you're being self-centred when in fact you're trying to empathize, which can annoy people. Neurodivergent people are likely to fixate over criticism, which might be why the idea has become so popular and spread so easily online.

Dealing with sceptics and trolls

Sadly, the growth of the online community, especially among women, has led to a backlash against neurodivergence. Every few weeks, a writer or vlogger who gets paid to wind people up writes or says something nasty about how ADHD isn't real or is over-diagnosed, or uses neurodivergence as a reason to have a go at a group of people they don't like. Not directly reacting to these, either by linking or screenshotting, is one of the best things you can do for your wellbeing. It means the publisher doesn't get money from clicks, and the article doesn't upset more people.

The only time I react to nasty articles is if they make very specific claims in public that are misleading and might directly put people off getting the help they need. Editors sometimes ask for people to go on radio shows and respond to arguments. You do not need to do this in order to have a career and it's perfectly possible to argue with myths without giving these people your personal attention.

Being trolled can be anything from annoying to amusing to physically frightening. The first time it happened to me, I spent the next two hours shaking. I've had to ask prominent tweeters who attract lots of trolls not to share my tweets, and I know of writers who've been prescribed anti-anxiety medication specifically to deal with trolling. Happily, responsible websites and apps are doing ever more to help users shut out trolls, so you can peacefully create content without someone called Roger43832 popping into your replies to tell you neurodivergence doesn't exist, or medication is bad, or you shouldn't be drinking that glass of wine you posted a photo of. Some trolling accounts are bots, although even the real ones are so lacking in imagination it's hard to tell the difference. A tiny minority of the more dedicated trolls will quote evidence of research studies they say prove their arguments, none of which proves what they say it does.

If you feel you have to respond to a troll, you could just

take on board a nugget of wisdom I once saw online, which said something like: 'Never to spend time arguing with someone you can remove from your life at the touch of a button.'

Privacy issues around story sharing

Sharing your own story about neurodivergence often leads to sharing information about other people in your life. I won't go into the intricacies of privacy law here because eating cardboard would be more exciting. But if you're writing a book or an article where you refer to others, you'll need their written permission, or you need to make sure they can't be identified. I've done so in this book.

This doesn't apply to personal social media accounts as such. However, posting about other people on social media is probably second to religion as a cause of arguments in the world. Years ago, I ran a personal blog that occasionally featured amusing stories and witty asides about my friends, as well as snippets from our conversations. I veered between believing I wasn't important enough that they would care, believing they would be flattered, and simply getting caught up in the need to vent so that nothing else seemed to matter. In fact, several people did care quite a lot, and didn't find my mentions flattering.

Much later, I learned that neurodivergence was part of the reason for all of this, especially my tendency to vent first and then think later.

One way to handle this when you're writing about other people is to apply something journalists call The Newspaper Test. Ask yourself: *'How would I feel if someone wrote this about me and put it on the front of a newspaper?'* If the answer is 'Not very pleased', don't put it on social media, or make sure they don't know it's them.

I covered whether and when to tell others about someone else's neurodivergence more generally back in Chapter 4, so head there if you missed it.

Final thoughts

My final tip about story sharing is from one of the first events where I spoke about dyspraxia.

I don't remember which one exactly, but I remember talking to a woman who asked whether I was a medical professional. 'No,' I replied. 'I'm just a writer.'

She corrected me: 'Never say "just". We need people like you.'

She was absolutely right, and it was great advice to me about learning to be kinder to myself. The next chapter is all about this.

CHAPTER 6: A QUICK RECAP

- People share their story for different reasons, but most are looking for connection.
- Ways of sharing your story can be divided into creating your own content and working with other organizations. There are pros and cons to both.
- Story sharing is more than sharing your story at a one-off event, it can include consultancy and research.
- All stories about neurodivergence are important. You are not 'just' or 'only' an anything.

CHAPTER 7

Being Kind to Your Mind

Or 'This Can't be "Growing Pains" Anymore!'

The internet is full of videos and posts by neurodivergent people trying to help each other be more productive. If you follow any other dyspraxic, ADHD or autistic people online, it's likely your feeds are flooded with tips from everywhere on how to make daily life easier: from managing money and time to cleaning and organizing your space. Of course, these practical tips are vital for anyone who struggles with executive dysfunction. We all need to get certain things done to stay alive and very few of us can afford to retreat to a mountain spa to take care of ourselves after a diagnosis. After years of endlessly talking about my struggles just to find a name for how I experienced the world, and then more years of feeling that just one name didn't cover it, I was relieved to find lots of online advice about how to *actually do things* from people who *actually* understood why it wasn't that easy.

However, in all the years I'd spent hating myself – affecting my ability to find regular work or a permanent home – hundreds of tips on how to clean my floor or organize my sock draw weren't all I needed. What I also needed were helpful, reframing versions of the punishing things I'd been saying to myself time and time again for years and years about my inability to get things done, and the anxiety that went with trying to do them. This chapter is about how I'm rewriting the script and learning to talk to myself more kindly.

An important reminder here: I'm not a therapist or coach, but I *am* someone who's experienced being a client of both. Later in this chapter I'll also explain what they are and how they're different and give some suggestions on what to look for in one as a neurodivergent person.

Recognizing your inner critic

Another important thing to note here is that learning to be kinder to yourself can take a long time. Like 'love your body' (more on that later), self-esteem tips can sometimes seem like a demand and become another thing to be cruel to ourselves about. Or as I once said to someone, 'I hate how I hate myself!' The tips that follow are a work-in-progress, not an instant recipe.

Reframing self-talk (or 'shushing your brain goblins')

My editor suggested I call this section 'reframing self-talk' but you might prefer something more playful. One person I know calls her self-critical thoughts 'brain goblins'.

- **Cruel version:** 'It's good to be scared, it helps you get things done.'
- **Kind version:** 'Fear does the *exact opposite of helping you get things done*.'

Throughout my teens and twenties, every self-improvement

article or book I came across seemed to start by assuring me that fear and self-criticism were actually good and useful. I read story after story about how adrenaline is the reason actors give cracking performances or politicians do the best speeches. Fear and self-criticism, like most things, *can* be useful *in moderation*. But my experience of them – and probably yours – isn't moderate. Telling someone who reads books about how to manage their anxiety that it's good to be scared is like telling someone who's trapped inside a burning building that it's good to be warm. I clung to this for years, despite mounting evidence that fear wasn't the reason I did anything and only got in the way of doing things (see below).

- **Cruel version:** 'You always sign up for things, then end up feeling too scared to do them and trying to chicken out!'
- **Kind version:** 'Your brain doesn't have what it needs to keep you consistently motivated and focused. It tries to make up for this by flooding you with fear.'

For decades, feeling debilitatingly anxious in the run up to events was a confusing, unexplainable pattern of life for me and for the few people I let see it: from crying all the way to Glastonbury and turning around at the gate, to pulling out of weekends away with days or hours to go, to taking an unplanned year off before university and then repeatedly nearly abandoning my place altogether right up until the day I finally arrived. Sometimes I knew what I was scared of, at other times I had no idea and just came out with all sorts of baffling reasons for why I suddenly didn't want to do something or go somewhere. Later, I identified as dyspraxic and anxious, which was closer to the truth, but didn't fully explain this – especially when the upcoming task or event had little to do with dexterity. After I was medicated for ADHD, I finally understood properly what had been going on in my brain for so long.

Unmedicated ADHD brains use up dopamine too fast, so we lack consistent motivation, even for the things we supposedly want to do, like going to big events. For some ADHDers, the brain tries to make up for this by flooding us with fear and stress signals to motivate us as the event gets closer, which does the opposite and makes us anxious. Our uneven abilities also make it easy to justify our feelings and find reasons for not doing things. To others, this looks as if we sign up for things unthinkingly and then selfishly try to chicken out. The criticism adds to our anxiety. Like most of my neurodivergent traits, I was led to assume I'd grow out of it. ('You're a 32-year-old adult, you need to sort this out,' a spectacularly unhelpful duty doctor at Accident & Emergency said to me once, looking at my medical notes.)

Instead, I had an ever-present mental list of things I wouldn't attempt doing and places I wouldn't attempt going because the thought of getting attacked by the usual brain goblins just beforehand was too unbearable. With medication, my overwhelm has practically disappeared and now I only feel its edges at certain times of the day or month when the effect wears off at the end of the day, or drops just before my period (see Chapter 9: Looking After Your Body). Most importantly, I now know that the way I felt for so long was down to my neurochemistry and not weakness, thoughtlessness, selfishness or anything else I could stop being just by trying hard enough.

This same pattern is why ADHDers famously rely on the fear of an imminent deadline to get things done.

- **Cruel version:** 'You should be more assertive!'
- **Kind version:** 'It's harder to be assertive sometimes because your body and brain don't work like others. And you don't have to be assertive all the time.'

If you've ever asked me what I think of Guinness cake, or lettuce as a main meal, or the government in power, you would not describe me as someone who has trouble knowing my own mind or standing up for myself. Nor would you if you had watched me give a speech or play Scrabble.

I also struggle to make decisions on the spot, like choose a parking space or a dish on a menu, or even where to sit down. I would trust a cat's sense of direction over mine. I feel self-conscious about doing certain things in front of others. This version of me is the one that lives in people's minds and tends to look as if I'm not assertive.

These things are nothing to do with being weak-willed but to do with ADHD and dyspraxia, which mean I process information more slowly. Now that I know this, I've found ways to work with it. Sometimes this can mean finding ways to speed up decision-making. For example, when I go to a restaurant I might book ahead and look at the menu beforehand so I can order quickly and focus on the conversation rather than trying to do both. Sometimes it means slowing a situation down. For example, if a street seller hits me with a sales pitch, I'll firmly let them know I don't make decisions about money on the spot, rather than trying to take it all in and getting battered into something I don't understand.

And sometimes, I'm happy just to let someone else decide. I once read that if someone offers you a choice, you should always give an opinion and never say you don't mind. I disagree. There's nothing wrong with saying you don't mind or have no opinion, if you genuinely don't, especially if it's a very simple decision.

While it's good to do what you can to protect yourself from harm, it's also important to remember that no amount of strength or sass – literally or metaphorically – is guaranteed to stop you ever being hurt or taken advantage of in life and that these things can happen to anybody at any time. 'Empowering' advice that just plays on your fear is to be avoided.

- **Cruel version:** 'Never put things off or do them at the last minute!'
- **Kind version:** 'Most things can be done quickly or last minute and lots of things are designed to be. Knowing which ones can't be done quickly comes with experience.'

We've never lived in a culture with instant access to so much. I remember someone who'd grown up in the seventies describing to me how his dad would spend weeks intricately planning a two-hour day trip to the seaside, poring over paper maps and traffic reports and organizing a picnic for the journey. Nowadays, last-minute trips are a booming industry, and tasks that once took weeks can be done in a couple of clicks or taps. Despite this, many of us still grow up feeling there's something superior about doing everything as far as possible in advance, especially as we probably had parents and grandparents who grew up before most of today's time-saving tech existed, and for whom tech is the opposite of time-saving.

When I was a chronic procrastinator, I used to fantasize about non-procrastination, as if replying to my emails within the hour was the equivalent of two weeks on a tropical island. Making life easier for yourself isn't about expecting to be able to do everything as soon as you possibly can, it's about getting to know which things you can do quickly or spontaneously, and which need more planning.

For example, once upon a time, form-filling meant weeks of planning and literal paperwork. Now thanks to online forms and autofill, plenty can be filled out in the time it takes a kettle to boil. On the other hand, I know I cannot and will probably never be able to quickly whip up a meal for several people. And I know when not to 'just quickly' try to squeeze in a task, because it's likely to result in me not leaving my desk for the next two hours.

Similarly, putting off opening emails can be sensible, even if they're important. For example, you might prefer to open exam results or medical letters at a time when there'll be someone around to help you deal with the information if you need to.

- **Cruel version:** 'You're too obsessed with this thing! It's bad for you! Think of something else instead!'
- **Kind version:** 'You find it difficult to control your attention. This doesn't mean that you're bad, or what you pay attention to is bad.'

Like many ADHDers and autistic people who grew up unrecognized, when I hyperfocused on something or someone, I often got the message that the object of my hyperfocus was the problem and the solution was to move on to a new interest. But my underlying attention problem meant that with every new interest, I ended up feeling as if I'd replaced one problem with another.

Obviously, if you're hyperfocused on something that's directly harmful to you or others, a different interest will be better for you – alongside appropriate help. But just labelling an interest as bad or letting go of it doesn't help to manage hyperfocus; it only moves it onto something else. I know I'll always be someone who hyperfocuses. But understanding it's what's happening to me can help me 'catch' it before it becomes too unmanageable.

- **Cruel version:** 'If you can't even..., how are you ever going to be able to...?'
- **Kind version:** 'With the right support, you can do both. Or it won't matter if you can't.'

Some years ago, there was a support organization called the Developmental Adult Neurodiversity Association (DANDA) for neurodivergent adults. Although it sadly disbanded, I remember a sentence from the website that said something like: 'Neurodivergence can make philosophy feel like an actual walk in the park and make an actual walk in the park feel impossible.'

I couldn't put it better.

- **Cruel version:** 'It's not normal to keep feeling like this, why can't you just move on?'
- **Kind version:** 'Certain events are hard for anyone to deal with, but being neurodivergent can also make it harder.'

In certain situations, having a brain that can hyperfocus and link ideas quickly has been an asset for me. Sadly, being affected by two sudden deaths of people close to me within three years before the age of 30 turned that brain into what could be described as a punishment device the cruellest minds in the world could not have dreamed up. In one case, although I only knew the person who died a short time, we coincidentally shared many links to places, which meant his death turned perfectly neutral facts about my life into constant roving reminders. My grief triggers (or 'sudden arrows' as the writer Julian Barnes (2015) calls them) have included any mention of where my dad grew up and went to school, the European city where my parents met and married, Brexit, social media, several popular news programmes, most songs released between 1967 and 1997, and neurodivergence itself.

Another reason I discovered it can be hard for neurodivergent people to move on from events is a particular type of fixation known as *perseveration* or 'getting stuck'. Perseveration is most obvious in very young children: when things don't go right for them, kids tend to fixate on trying to change what they can't change rather than being able to accept it and move on. They might keep going back to look for a lost toy, insisting it 'must' be there, or keep asking the same question over and over again hoping for a better answer. Or in the case of my three-year-old self, try to make a set of immovable toy plastic figurines turn around to face the other way.

Adults can also react in this sort of way after a difficult or traumatic event. Grown-up perseveration can look like going over and over things we could have done or said, or feeling as if something difficult or impossible 'has' to happen for something in our lives to feel resolved. The three-year-old who went spare trying to move immovable plastic figurines grew into the 30-year-old me who spent years going over feelings and speculating in my head. Neurodivergent people can be more prone to this kind of reaction after difficult events because we tend to fixate anyway.

As you might have guessed, my way of dealing with difficult fixations has been trying to turn them into something positive. Rather than hating myself for feeling the way I did, I created grief rituals which slowly helped give meaning to time and purpose to my life.

- **Cruel version:** 'It's always one step forward and two back. You're your own worst enemy!'
- **Kind version:** 'You don't have consistent levels of the brain chemicals you need to function so it's hard to make consistent progress in your life.'

Making good choices in your life and turning good choices into good outcomes both rely on good executive functions. When you don't have them, or know why, or know what to do about it, you get the feeling of stuckness I wrote about in Chapter 1, which leads to a vicious circle of self-blame. It's like walking along a never-ending path and finding the path is blocked every few miles, so instead of moving forward, it feels as if you're endlessly looking for ways around this and blaming yourself for not moving fast enough.

I have tried to write books countless times, but never finished them because I lost the motivation and the ability to organize information, and hated myself for what felt like yet another waste of time. Now I know why this happens to me, I can look for support to help me stay motivated and organized.

- **Cruel version:** 'You're an adult! You should be able to do things for yourself by now!'
- **Kind version:** 'You need support from others to help you do more for yourself.'

When I reached the age of 18, people assumed that simply being 18 meant I should be expected to do everything adults were expected to do. For neurodivergent and/or disabled people, being able to do things for ourselves isn't something that just happens. In fact, assuming the magic day would arrive when I'd just grow up and manage anything by myself rather than having support to manage things was why I'd ended up almost totally dependent on others for everything. The more I tried to do without support, the more I struggled, and so in the end the less I tried to do, the more I regressed. Now I accept that the way my brain works means that independence is something I have to be helped to achieve. It's no more immature to need someone to hold you accountable in order to get things done than it is to need help climbing the stairs or need to turn on audio description to follow a film. Not understanding and allowing myself those needs didn't help me grow up, it stopped me enjoying life at all.

- **Cruel version:** 'You should have...' 'If only...'
- **Kind version:** 'You did what you did based on what you knew and didn't know at the time...'

If only I'd known I was neurodivergent when I was younger, leaving home wouldn't have been so hard. If only I'd hyperfocused on people who actually wanted to pay me for my skills when I was younger, instead of offering myself for free. If only I was interested in things that made more money. If only I'd asked for support in that interview, I'd have got a job that was better for me instead of completely the wrong one. If only I'd resigned before I was pushed out. If only I'd known anything about how to run a business before I tried to. If only I'd done all those things, I'd have been happier and met happier people.

All these 'if onlys' and 'shoulds' have made me the person I am, and all these have happened because I didn't know who I was then. This is true for every neurodivergent person and, sometimes, things have to get worse before you can find the support to get better…

Finding support for your neurodivergence

The three main types of support for neurodivergence are **talking therapy**, **coaching** and **medication**. In my experience, most neurodivergent people benefit from at least one and often two or three of these. In my case, each one has highlighted the need for the other. The rest of this chapter is about counselling and coaching. The next chapter is about medication.

Counselling or talking therapy

Someone once said to me that finding the right therapist is like looking for the right relationship: it takes a lot of wrong ones to find the right one. I can eminently relate to this. I first went to see a counsellor just after my post A-level breakdown. Back then, going to counselling or therapy was seen as less ordinary than it is today, and online therapy was unimaginable, so being a non-driver in a small town meant little choice in who you saw. I can remember dropping my voice whenever I told the reception desk who I was there to see, and hating being made to wait in the single chair outside the special corridor. My counsellor seemed strangely surprised I didn't look happy or comfortable to be there. She soon recognized that the short-term problems I presented with were part of a much bigger one, but we didn't end up finding a solution together.

For more than a decade after that, I went on having handfuls of whatever therapy I could get for free everywhere I went, because I kept having problems I either felt I couldn't tell people about, or didn't want to keep telling them about again and again. Eventually, I reached the point of being ineligible for any because my problems were either too complicated or not complicated enough. Someone at a local centre once asked me: 'But why do you need our help when you know you're dyspraxic?'; which is a bit like a dentist asking why you keep coming back to them when you know you have teeth.

Fortunately, the counsellor I saw at the lowest point in my life also happened to be the best fit I'd ever experienced. Three years of weekly counselling and then another short stint of coaching ultimately led to my complete diagnosis and medication.

Although therapy is, quite rightly, much less stigmatized than it used to be, there's still an unhelpful myth that people with good friends don't need professional help to talk through their feelings. Some neurodivergent people do lack good friends and deserve support to talk about things if they want to. Some of us may feel we lack good friends, even if that's not the case. Most importantly, we might have had experiences in our lives that need more support than a friend can give without the friendship becoming imbalanced. Healthy friendships are a two-way thing; therapy is one-way and all about helping you. A therapist should listen and guide you towards what's best for you. Unlike friendships, therapy has spoken and written boundaries, including an agreed beginning and end. This can make it a really good idea if you struggle with unlabelled relationships, or relationships that seem to revolve around either your problems or the other person's.

While therapy before a diagnosis tends to be about trying to 'name the problem' or solve one problem after another, therapy after a diagnosis can help you move beyond this to understanding and feeling better about yourself. Neurodivergent people are well represented in therapy rooms, not just as clients but as practitioners too. An increasing number of therapists are openly neurodivergent and many of them offer therapy remotely to clients all over the world. A simple search for 'neurodivergent specialist therapist' or the Association of Neurodivergent Therapists should bring up suggestions.

The best therapy I've had in my life has helped me with the following aspects:

- **Feel my feelings somewhere safe and structured:** If you're constantly being distracted by feelings that have nowhere to go, it's very difficult to do anything else.

- **Find a middle ground between thinking everything is either my fault or someone else's:** This is a common struggle when you find it difficult to regulate your emotions. Often, when giving advice, well-meaning friends or family will either tell you what you want to hear ('I'm sure she's not avoiding you, she's probably just busy!') or enforce your worst fears with their own speculation ('Maybe she doesn't want to see you because you remind her too much of her ex!'), neither of which is necessarily helpful. A good therapist should help you work through your fears and look for answers where possible. Any therapist should also help you recognize situations you're not to blame for at all, like if someone is abusing you, especially if they're using neurodivergent traits to justify doing it.

- **Recognize trauma:** Trauma is caused by experiencing something frightening, distressing or stressful, either a single event or repeatedly. Symptoms of trauma can include nightmares, flashbacks, intrusive thoughts and trying to avoid reminders of the trauma that interfere with your life. Being neurodivergent or from a marginalized group doesn't automatically mean someone is traumatized. However, it's increasingly understood that neurodivergent people may be more likely to experience trauma, especially if we've lived for a long time without recognition or support. This can be because of directly experiencing traumatic situations, like abuse or violence, or it can come from experiencing ordinary situations as traumatic, like driving, exercising in public, giving birth, being in a noisy or busy environment, being in an unsupportive workplace, or trying to do everyday tasks.

    Realizing you've booked a train for the wrong day isn't traumatic for most people, but if it reminds you of making mistakes at work that led to you losing your job and home, it might be, and might lead to a reaction that makes your worried neighbour believe you've been murdered (sorry, neighbours). A counsellor or therapist can help you recognize you've had trauma and offer you specific treatments to help you manage it.

    A therapist who specializes in working with ADHD clients with trauma briefly explained how the brain handles memories. If someone asks you what you had to eat on a random day last year, you probably can't remember. This is because our less impactful memories are stored at the back of the brain, and the more impactful ones are at the front. These can include nice memories, or traumatic ones. Trauma therapy is about moving traumatic memories from the front to the back of the brain, so they feel less intrusive.

- **Understand how certain patterns in relationships relate to my neurodivergence, especially fixation:** Working with therapists who are neurodivergent themselves can be helpful when it comes to managing fixations. Some neurotypical therapists have made me feel more trapped by fixation by seeming to be judgemental, distracting me with too many side questions, or pushing me too hard to imagine myself in hypothetical situations. These can all be difficult if you're neurodivergent, especially when you're talking about something you feel very emotional about.

- **Understand when talking about something alone won't resolve a situation and I need to make decisions or take specific actions:** For some people, this is the point they decide to look for a diagnosis. If you already have one, it might be the point where you look for coaching or medication.

Coaching for neurodivergence

Alongside the many thousands of general life coaches and business coaches, there is a growing industry of coaches, usually people with lived experience, who specialize in supporting neurodivergent adults. A simple search for 'ADHD coaching', or asking around in ADHD community groups, will bring up many names.

Some staff at ADHD diagnostic centres also work as coaches,[1] and there's a directory of coaches at ADHD UK[2] who work with clients all over the world. Although counselling and coaching are sometimes seen as more or less the same thing, coaching is something different. Coaching is about using your understanding of yourself to achieve long-term goals, whereas counselling is about understanding yourself and your feelings. What that means can also look very different depending on those goals and your coach's approach.

Like counselling, I have a varied history with coaching stretching back a long way. My first couple of experiences were negative because of my incomplete understanding of myself (not knowing that I had ADHD alongside my dyspraxia) and my unrealistic expectations (see below).

Since my ADHD diagnosis, I have used coaching alongside medication, mostly to reach specific goals in my life, including the book you're reading. Here are some ways coaching can help:

- **Finding new ways to do things that work for you:** There are lots of productivity tips online, but working with a coach one to one can help you find those that specifically work for your situation.

- **Giving you accountability, especially on long tasks or projects:** I have found that sending sections of the books to a writing coach helps me keep track of time and keeps my writing clean. This means I don't end up spending uncontrolled amounts of time doing minor edits or writing a particularly interesting or emotionally triggering section.

    Accountability can be useful for more routine tasks

---

1   At the ADHD Centre in the UK, for example (www.adhdcentre.co.uk/cognitive-behavioural-therapy-cbt).
2   https://store.adhduk.co.uk/adhd-uk-coaches

too, like helping you remember to eat, sleep and take care of yourself in other ways.

- **Helping you** with planning and organizing whether it's specific tasks, like organizing your home or work space, or more long-term goals.

- **Supporting you with specific tasks you find hard:** For many ADHDers, this usually means support with admin. If you're dyspraxic, a coach or support worker may also be able to help with some practical tasks like cleaning, preparing food and repairing things.

See below for a checklist to use if you're looking for either a counsellor or coach, and for more about finding free or low-cost support.

What to look for in a counsellor or coach

A good therapist or coach should:

- **Be upfront and realistic about their qualifications and experience:** Counsellor, therapist and coach aren't protected titles, which means anyone can call themselves one without any qualifications. For coaching, specific qualifications might not matter as much as relevant experience. For any kind of counselling or therapy, they most definitely matter. Always check that someone is accredited by a professional body and that their organization isn't a pyramid scheme or a therapy cult. A quick internet search should tell you all these things. If someone uses the title 'Doctor', make sure you know whether they're a medical doctor or someone with a PhD: a PhD only qualifies someone to work with your brain if it involves clinical work as well as research. Most neurodiversity coaches aren't doctors, so always check with your health provider that any health or diet-based tips are safe for you.

Some coaches blur the line between coaching and counselling. If a business or life coach starts talking about your childhood or using hypnotherapy techniques, that's counselling, and they should be qualified to do it.

If you're looking for a coach to help you find work or build up a business from scratch, look for one who has specifically helped people in these situations and preferably with your skills. Although lots of ADHD coaches advertise themselves as offering work-related support, lots of these are geared towards people who are in work, or earning a regular income from running a business, and may not be a good investment if you're struggling financially.

- **Ideally have worked with neurodivergent clients before and preferably understand different presentations and challenges:** Back when I first got my dyspraxia diagnosis, coaching organizations which said they supported dyspraxic or neurodivergent adults were often really set up to support dyslexics, or autistic men working in tech jobs. Although this doesn't seem the case so much now, it's good to make sure the support any person or organization is offering is for your type of neurodivergence. If you're not sure, they shouldn't mind you asking.

- **Make it easy for you to book, pay for and cancel sessions:** Any neurodivergent-friendly business should offer contactless payment, online booking systems and clear cancellation policies, written and spoken.

- **Be led by what's happening to you right now, and not

go over your childhood beyond where it's helpful: Of course, things that have happened to you when you were younger will have shaped you, and the younger you are, the more that is likely to be the case. If you've had experiences like abuse or poverty, of course exploring these can be helpful. But going over my childhood just for the sake of it, or with the aim of looking for a single person or incident to blame, has never helped me and has even been counterproductive. I've heard from people whose neurodivergence or other important diagnoses were missed well into adulthood because all their problems were blamed on the size or gender balance of their family, or them being an only/middle/oldest child, or similar. No family setup is inherently 'ideal' or 'perfect', and the reasons why our parents had fewer or more children often explain more of our lives rather than the choice itself.

- **Use social media in a way you're comfortable with:** If social media is a big part of your life and work, make sure your counsellor or coach understands this, as some still don't use it or believe it's bad for people. Equally, therapists or coaches shouldn't post about their clients on social media, even anonymously, without their clear consent.

Finding counselling or coaching on a budget

Counselling and coaching are often expensive, but don't have to be. Depending on where you live, finding support for little or nothing might be easier than finding a professional diagnosis, without waiting for years or paying, and you shouldn't even need a professional diagnosis to access support. I'm going to assume from you reading this that 1) You've heard of the best-known national crisis lines or listening services in the UK or your country, 2) You're considered either 'too ill' or 'not ill enough' for more help from the NHS or whatever healthcare is free in your country.

Online therapy
Since online therapy became more popular during the Covid pandemic, many private therapists offer sessions online, which often reduces the cost. Therapists, especially those who are neurodivergent themselves, are often sensitive to the high cost of living and may also offer pay-what-you-can rates to low-income clients.

If you can't find an affordable, neurodivergent-friendly therapist privately, small, local charities that provide general counselling are the next most likely places to find long-term help. They may not advertise heavily, either to limit demand or because they're run by volunteers or part-timers and don't have the money or time to spend on promoting themselves, so finding them can take a bit of work or word-of-mouth recommendation.

If it's specifically coaching you're looking for rather than therapy, many coaches are self-employed or work for organizations that specifically support neurodivergent adults. There are very few specific to dyspraxia, but more for ADHD and autism.

Peer support
If it's too difficult to find good, low-cost coaching from a paid service, or if you prefer something with more of a community feel, peer support can be a great alternative for supporting you with some aspects of neurodivergence. Like coaching, peer support schemes are often run by people with lived experience and promoted on social media or online forums, and are often online based. Unlike coaching, they're often free, very low cost or operate on a pay-what-you-can basis. They usually meet at set intervals, like weekly or monthly. They're particularly helpful for

ADHDers as they can help you build structure into your life and give you accountability. For example, a group might have weekly meetings where you can set and review goals or break big goals into smaller ones. They may also help you with accountability by running body-doubling sessions for accountability.

Body doubling means working on a task while you're with other people or someone watches you while you do a task. It's a more supportive, fun and less demeaning version of having your mum or your boss come and stand over you while you do something so that you'll finally remember to do it. Body-doubling sessions often take place over video calls or livestream so you can body double with anyone in the world. Peer support can help support the effects of medication. It's also popular among ADHDers who are unmedicated or who don't respond well to medication.

Final thoughts

I hope this chapter has helped you feel kinder to your mind. Getting the best emotional support, especially from a professional, is often about finding the right level of support for your situation in the moment. Some services support people in crisis, while others are about gradual change and long-term commitment. If you need help urgently, there's a list of crisis support organizations in the back of the book.

This chapter has been all about taking care of your brain and how we can be kind to ourselves including in our self-talk. For many ADHDers, taking medication for ADHD is an important part of this. If you're starting medication, or considering it, the next chapter is for you. Otherwise, head to Chapter 9 for more about looking after your body.

CHAPTER 7: A QUICK RECAP

- Finding out you're neurodivergent is about learning to be kind to yourself as well as learning new ways of doing things.
- Counselling and coaching can help you with being kinder to yourself. Counselling can help you understand your feelings and make sense of your past. Coaching can help you build a future.
- Counselling and coaching can be helpful with or without medication. There's more about medication in the next chapter.

CHAPTER 8

How Medication Works for Me

This chapter is about my experience with stimulant medication as a woman with ADHD and dyspraxia, and is aimed at adults who are starting or considering it. To be prescribed stimulants in the UK and most other countries, you'll need a diagnosis of ADHD from a doctor, and Chapters 1 and 2 have more on diagnosis. There's currently no medication approved to treat dyspraxia, or DCD, as it's medically known. However, my own personal experience is that stimulants also help with hand-eye coordination. More about that in a moment...

My number one tip for anyone considering medication is not to be put off by myths, or the fear that it won't work. If my medication had been offered to me 20 years earlier, those 20 years might have looked very different. My first couple of days on it (naturally, after weeks of putting it off...) were like the sun coming out after a long winter. Although the effect fluctuates more now, even a less-good day on medication is infinitely better than my life before. I'd always been told that any medication should always be a last resort, that relying on it was a bad thing and – an old family favourite – *'There is no magic pill!'* Medication isn't a 'magic pill'. But it's as close to one as I'll ever get, and I'd like everyone else who might benefit from something that's been this life-changing for me to know about it.

I'm not going to include any statistics here about the effectiveness of medication, and for the same reason I haven't included any about how many assessments led to a diagnosis. Even if I said it worked for a hundred per cent of people, there'd still be people reading this and wondering: 'But what if I'm the first person in the world it *doesn't* work for?!' And saying it works for X per cent of people doesn't help if you're in the minority of people it hasn't worked for. What I am including here is the general medical advice I've been given about medication, and my lived experience of taking it. Though I often joke about wanting to meet the inventor of my medication and offer him or her an indecent thank you, I don't work for any pharmaceutical company, and nobody is paying me to say any of this. As with any treatment, co-occurring health needs can affect how you respond to medication.

> Always see a specialist before trying medication or making any changes to your medication.

How medication works and can help

For the brain to do anything, brain cells, or **neurons**, have to pass messages to each other, called **neurotransmission**. They do this by releasing chemicals called **neurotransmitters**. These are the all-important chemicals I mentioned at the beginning of the book, **dopamine** and **noradrenaline**, which help us with executive functions like managing our attention, memory, motor skills and emotions. It's thought that ADHD and/or dyspraxic brains don't release enough neurotransmitters, or the neurotransmitters get sucked back up too quickly, so those messages don't get through, giving us the difficulties we have. Medication works by either helping the brain produce more neurotransmitters or slowing down the re-uptake so information can get through and our difficulties improve.

The most common medication used to treat ADHD in the UK and US is known as stimulants. There are different types, and they go by different names in different countries. I won't go into the details here, but you can find lots of helpful information online. Just make sure it comes from a reputable source. Non-stimulants help in similar ways and are sometimes used for people who don't get on with stimulants.

Unlike other drugs, which work instantly and stay in the body for several days, most stimulants take two hours to work and wear off gradually at the end of the day.

Although stimulants are mainly recognized as ways to improve focus, they often also improve other executive functions, which can help you with a great deal else. For me, the most life-changing impact has been the ability to handle my emotions better. More on that in a moment. ADHDers who struggle with emotional regulation are often prescribed antidepressants, but these can make executive dysfunction worse in some people, which in my case led to the not-ideal scenario of being more forgetful but appearing less bothered about it.

'ADHD medication works for dyspraxia too!'

A few months into taking my ADHD medication, I started to notice that as well as all the benefits I'd hoped for, something else was changing in me. At the times when the medication was most active in my body, I was finding everyday tasks like making lunch a lot easier than usual. One lunchtime, I even tried out a new recipe for soup in a heatwave when it was nearly 40 degrees. (For comparison, on a bad day when it's *not* 40 degrees, my dyspraxic hands can struggle to put together a simple snack.) I told my doctor, who confirmed that, yes, it was likely my dyspraxic difficulties were being improved by medication too. In the 15 years since my dyspraxia diagnosis, I'd never once been told that any medication could specifically help with this.

At the time I'm writing, there's no written medical evidence I can find to support my experience, or evidence of ADHD medication being recognized as a treatment for dyspraxia. This is sadly unsurprising given the lack of research into adult dyspraxia full stop. However, since both ADHD and dyspraxia are thought to be related to how the body handles dopamine, it makes sense that taking medication which gives us the dopamine we lack can help with both. As our understanding of ADHD increases, I hope our understanding of dyspraxia catches up.

'So what's the catch?'

- **Medication doesn't work for everyone, depending on who you are:** Like any medication, other health conditions and any other types of medication you take can affect how well ADHD medication works for you, or make it less suitable. Your doctor should talk to you about your medical history before prescribing you anything.

- **The 'period drop':** In women and those people assigned female at birth, the effect of stimulants tends to drop during the second half of the menstrual cycle because of hormonal changes. There is more about handling periods in the next chapter.

- **Stigma around medication:** There are myths and misunderstandings about taking medication for ADHD (see below), largely because it is a controlled drug and because of the stigma that exists towards brain-based medication in general.

Medication mythbusters

ADHD medication is NOT addictive OR 'the same' as street drugs

Saying that ADHD medication and speed or cocaine are basically the same thing because they're all stimulants is a bit like saying pineapples and mouldy bananas are basically the same thing because they're both fruit. Stimulants are called that because they increase motivation and energy. But unlike recreational drugs, prescription stimulants are also designed to focus and calm you rather than give you an intense high. Most prescription stimulants are slow acting, meaning the active ingredient is released gradually once it's in your body and you don't get an immediate buzz from it. The closest thing I've felt to a stimulant high is similar to the 'high' that comes from music or exercise. Both of those things mimic the way the medication works and help your brain to handle dopamine.

I never say any medication is impossible to abuse because, frankly, any substance on earth can probably be abused by someone sadly determined enough. But if you don't have a history of substance abuse, you're highly unlikely to abuse it, and, if you do, the right medication could help your recovery. Some ADHDers who've taken street drugs before being diagnosed and medicated say that the street drugs had a similar effect to legal medication and made them feel calm rather than high. The bottom line is that when you buy drugs off the street, you have no idea what you're getting, and a prescription will always be safer than a pill from a stranger that could be anything.

ADHD medication should NOT 'turn you into a zombie' or 'get rid of your personality'

Do I seem like someone who's been turned into a zombie? I hope not.

Medication improves executive function, and having either strong or weak executive function brings both strengths and problems to your life. Weaker executive function can make you creative, but it is harder to use that creativity in the most helpful way and you may also feel as if your head is full of bees. This is why creative people are stereotyped as intense and chaotic, and why ADHDers tend to be stereotyped as people who do creative jobs. Very strong executive function can make you well organized and efficient but it can also be hard to think creatively or be spontaneous. This is why professions that rely on logic, routine and sequential thinking, like science and technology, are stereotyped as being boring, and why many ADHDers worry that taking medication for their executive functioning will change who they are. Medication isn't about turning you into a robot or a human spreadsheet, it's about finding a more comfortable balance between these extremes. If it makes you feel flat and zombie-like, your dose may be too high. If it does nothing, your dose might be too low.

The reason medication can make some people feel like a different person is that a lot of our personality develops out of our unsupported ADHD. Listening to music, eating chocolate and scrolling social media – three things which have defined my life – have all compensated for the dopamine my unmedicated brain was using up too fast, and being medicated meant I spent noticeably less time doing them. My whole adult life had revolved around defensive humour about my inability to get things done. When sending emails or taking a trip to the corner shop stopped feeling so much like a mission to Mars, my life changed. Having the motivation to organize trips out and the confidence to handle the admin without worrying I'd make some mistake made me more proactive and assertive. I could see how my unrelated emotions and attention could sometimes make me seem self-involved and uncompromising, or how I took it personally if my intensity just wasn't matched.

Most of all, ADHD medication made me realize how much I'd relied on writing as a way to organize my feelings. When medication is in my body, I feel as if one way that it works is that it tries to protect me from those feelings so I can get on with other things, like a bouncer on the door telling those feelings that they can't come in. This is helpful for some writing, and for admin like filing invoices, and staying calm when travelling. It's less helpful when I'm writing something that relies on getting to those big feelings and memories. Sometimes, those memories rush back in at the end of the day once the medication has worn off: the so-called 'rebound' effect. Would I swap any of that for the ability to sit down and write at all? Absolutely not. Medication hasn't 'got rid' of my personality or my feelings. It's just turned down the volume of my personality and my feelings so I can work.

You DON'T have to put up with major long-term side effects from medication

Three of the most common side effects are nausea, reduced appetite, and reduced or increased sex drive. These can be annoying, but should go away sometime within the first few days to the first year. Some people, including me, get tics from their medication. The next chapter has more on this, and on all things to do with ADHD, dyspraxia and your body.

There is NO evidence to suggest that medication works differently in people without ADHD

ADHD medication works the same way whether you have ADHD

or not, just as painkillers work the same way whether you're in pain or not. But people who don't need it are unlikely to feel the benefit of it, just as it would be pointless to take a painkiller if you didn't need to.

There is NO rule on whether you should or shouldn't take breaks from medication. It depends on your lifestyle
The idea that you should take breaks from stimulants comes from the belief that they affect children's growth. The idea that you shouldn't comes from people's experiences with other medication. Unlike other psychiatric drugs, where missing a dose or stopping medication can be extremely dangerous, missing a day or two of stimulants shouldn't harm you. Some people prefer to take breaks from time to time because they find it hard to switch off from work or other responsibilities while taking them, especially in the early stages. Some chronic pain sufferers have told me they're able to nap on them. For some people, like parents of small children, taking breaks just isn't an option.

If you take medication breaks, you may find that stimulants start giving you nausea afterwards. This cleared up for me within a couple of months.

As my doctor says, when planning breaks: 'Pick your moment.' In my first year on medication, I took a break over my birthday weekend and ended up overwhelmed and weeping on Brighton Beach surrounded by concerned family. Breaks are best for me when I'm vegging out alone in familiar surroundings and nowhere near big occasions, or my period.

Healthy living isn't a substitute for medication
Exercise, eating well and living a healthy lifestyle are all good for you and will all help medication do its job better. They are all the more helpful if you aren't medicated for any reason. But they don't and will never work as efficiently as something designed to

do that job. You can't 'wellness' your way out of ADHD any more than you can anything else you take medication for.

Tips for your first week of stimulants and beyond

People often ask, 'How will I know if my medication is working? Can anything bad happen from taking it?'
The annoying but simple answer is: 'Trust me, you'll know if it is. In a good way.'

On my first medicated day, a Saturday in November, I went for two walks, read a whole book and didn't look at my phone from the morning until 6pm. On a normal day, I would have struggled to do even one of those things.

It's highly unlikely you'll react dangerously to medication. However, as with any medication, it's a good idea to start on a day you're not working and let someone else know you're taking it.

Your prescriber will usually start you on a low dose and gradually increase it to the average dose until you're stable. This is called titration. Whether a higher or lower dose works for you isn't to do with how 'severe' your ADHD or neurodivergence is; it's to do with the speed of your metabolism.

Try to take your medication as soon as possible after waking up and at the same time each day
No matter what else happens in a day, my morning medication routine always gives me the feeling of starting the day well and doing something. I associate medication with feeling calm and I cherish that feeling enough that, in my two-and-a-half years of being medicated, I've never forgotten to take a pill, even once. The more your body associates it with a positive outcome, the more likely you are to remember to take it. It's best to take

medication two hours before you start work and before 9am or else it can be difficult to sleep. If you work night shifts, talk to your prescriber about how to adjust this advice.

Try to take your medication with a decent-sized breakfast
It's important to eat breakfast with your medication, or you might feel nauseous/tired/moody later. Some people like to eat breakfast early, take their meds and then go back to bed for a couple of hours until they kick in. Others find that once they're awake, they're awake. If you forget to have enough food in the house in the morning, it's worth bulk-buying carb-y breakfast foods that don't go off, such as cereal, cereal bars or porridge.

Drink plenty of water and have some mints or toothpaste handy
Stimulants can often give you a dry mouth, which can lead to thirstiness and bad breath.

Try to avoid caffeine or orange juice when medication is most active in your body
Stimulants contain caffeine, and too much caffeine can lead to anxiety. The Vitamin C in orange juice can affect the efficacy of medication. I drink decaf in the morning and switch to regular tea in the afternoon. Similarly, I don't drink orange juice for breakfast, but wait until later in the day.

Try to snack during the day
Reduced appetite and increased focus can make it harder to eat lunch during the day. Snacks you can easily grab or eat a little bit of at a time (fruit, nuts, cereal bars) are your friend.

Go easy on alcohol
It should be safe to drink while you're on medication, but

binge-drinking and mixing drinks are best avoided, especially early on while your body adjusts to your medication. I tend to avoid gin specifically, as it can make me feel aggressive, especially when my medication is wearing off in the evenings.

Don't worry if your medication drops after the first few days
This is normal when you're on a starter dose and just means you're ready to increase your dose.

While you're on a low dose, try to order your repeat prescription a week before you run out
Pharmacies often don't have lower doses of medication in stock as not enough people take them, so it can take them a few days to order it.

Avoid having to split pills if you can
If your medication comes in quantities of, say, 30mg or 40mg and your prescriber wants to increase your dose from 30mg to 40mg after a couple of weeks, they may suggest you split pills to get the correct dose so you don't waste half a packet of lower-dose pills. However, dealing with fiddly amounts of white powder first thing in the morning can lead to a mess if you're dyspraxic, and leaving wraps of powdered foil and a store card next to the bedside table isn't ideal for anybody. If you want to save yourself the hassle and avoid your kitchen looking like the set of *Breaking Bad*, ask nicely if there's an alternative to pill splitting, especially if you don't live with anyone who can help you.

Don't up your dose any higher if your medication is working well
If you're getting on well with your medication, it's natural to think that increasing the dose is a good idea. But just like over-salting

your chips won't make them taste better, upping your medication dose too high won't make it work better. Upping my dose too high was like being swept off my feet by a dream lover who's suddenly turned nasty. Calm focus was replaced by weeping at the same time every day, raging PMS and unbearable sensory issues, which meant I could hear people's lips smacking. After two pretty horrible weeks I went back down a dose, where I've stayed ever since.

If medication doesn't work for you, or crashes...
I was lucky to respond well to the first medication I tried. For some people, it takes two or three different types to settle on one. Food, drink, hormones and weather extremes are the most likely things to affect how well medication works, or cause sudden mood crashes. Crashes can feel horrible, but thankfully rarely last more than an hour or two.

Travelling with medication
When I travel, I carry my medication in a dosette box and only take as much as I need for the time I'm away, plus one spare tablet. This means I have a spare tablet if one gets lost or dropped, but also means that if I lose the box, I don't lose too many tablets.

Dealing with pharmacists
Most pharmacists are nice people, and in my direct experience, one or two have been wonderfully helpful and sympathetic when there have been shortages of my medication (see below). Sadly, I've also experienced a minority who seem to treat controlled drug patients with uncalled-for hostility and suspicion. I actually complained to the head office of a large pharmacy chain after one of their staff refused me a prescription because she wrongly believed I was over-ordering, then shouted at me

and reduced me to tears in front of a queue of customers (and rapidly apologized when I went back with a man, too upset to speak for myself...). If anything like this happens to you, you have every right to ask for an apology. Since the incident, I use an online pharmacy whenever I can. This also handily avoids queuing, waiting and being exposed to other people's germs.

'Help! I can't stop hyperfocusing...!'

To quote my doctor once more: 'Medication gives you the focus. What you do with it is up to you.'

My chronic procrastination, the main reason I wanted medication, disappeared like magic as soon as the medication started to work, making me weep with gratitude (once it had worn off for the day and I could cry...). Over the first weeks and months, as my brain started to adjust to the medication, I found that my problem starting tasks was replaced by the opposite problem: I would get started on something and not be able to stop or finish. This is where other coping strategies like coaching come in. Coaching didn't work for me before I was medicated, because I lacked the underlying ability to focus and manage my emotions. For many medicated ADHDers, medication is like the foundations of a house: it gives you the basic structure you can build everything else around, especially if there are shortages of your medication.

Final thoughts

While I've been writing this book, there have been ongoing worldwide shortages of several of the most popular brands of stimulant medication. There are many reasons for this, including increased demand. I've lost several workdays to travelling ridiculous distances to find a pharmacy with my strength of medication in stock. Others have had to go without altogether or ration their medication to avoid doing so. While I hope the situation is different by the time you read this book, it's worth being aware that shortages are always possible. I now have a list saved on Google Maps of every pharmacy in every area I can get to for when they happen.

This is the only chapter that is specifically about medication and the only one for which you need a specific diagnosis for it to be personally relevant to you, though you may have friends or family it is useful for. The next chapter is about looking after your body in general.

CHAPTER 8: A QUICK RECAP

- Medication is usually prescribed for ADHD and may also help with dyspraxia. Although there isn't an approved medication for dyspraxia, in my personal experience, stimulant medication helps with both.
- It's understandable to feel nervous about taking medication, but don't be put off by myths and misunderstandings. Medication doesn't work for everyone with ADHD and might not be suitable for you, but it's safe and highly effective for many people.
- There are other, non-stimulant, medications available for ADHD. You'll be offered these if stimulants don't work for you.
- ADHD medication is a treatment, not a 'cure'. It is effective for as long as it's in your body, and wears off after 12–14 hours.

CHAPTER 9

Looking After Your Body

Or 'Why Didn't They Tell Us This at School?!'

As a woman, there's a good chance you haven't been told enough about how your body works at all, let alone how dyspraxia and ADHD affect the way you feel about it. Because of the little boy stereotypes around neurodivergence, there's still very little understanding or research into the relationship between our brains and our bodies.

This chapter looks at food (making it, buying it), drink and drugs, sleep beauty products, periods and hormones. This *isn't* a chapter about how to 'love your body' because I don't agree with forcing everyone to love their body, any more than I agree with encouraging everyone to hate it and try to make it live up to impossible beauty standards. But I do think that finding some pride in your body, and, most importantly, understanding how your body works, are all good things. As is knowing that there's someone else who does those things you can't talk to anyone about...

All bodies are different, and no body advice, no matter how

inclusive, can be right for everyone. Other disabilities and long-term health conditions and your relationship to your gender may, of course, affect your relationship with your body alongside neurodivergence. **Always talk to your health provider or a qualified person before making any diet or lifestyle changes.**

> Health conditions associated with neurodivergence: Certain health conditions are thought to be more common for neurodivergent people. There's a list of them with details of where to find information and support at the end of this book.

Neurodivergence and food (or 'Why it's easier for me to make you a wedding cake than a sandwich')

Once upon a time, I remember listening to my best friend laugh at how her little brother had broken a kettle by trying to boil stock cubes in it. Much later, I confessed to having done the same to a kettle by trying to boil milk in it as a timesaver (Food tip 1: Don't do that). From chopping food to timing food to juggling different tasks and kitchen distractions, having a neurodivergent brain, especially a dyspraxic one, can make one of the most essential parts of being alive into one of the most difficult. But over the years I've learned to manage making food for myself and others without too much damage to my surroundings. And sometimes even *enjoy* it.

Knowing my 'easy' and 'hard' or 'good' and 'bad' day foods
How well I cook depends on energy levels and how well my ADHD medication is working in my body. As I know that these things in turn depend heavily on where I'm at hormonally – more

on hormones very shortly – I tend to do most of my cooking from scratch in the early part of my cycle when planning ahead and doing things in the right order are easiest for me, and make enough leftovers for my bad days, when these abilities have left the building, or when I get caught in hyperfocus and end up eating late.

Making food is a classic example of the neurodivergent experience where tasks that sound 'harder' are actually easier than 'easy' ones. I explained why in an article I wrote a few years ago called 'Why I'd Rather Make You a Wedding Cake for You than a Sandwich' (Roper, 2020). The gist of it is that if you struggle with executive function, it's much easier to plan and follow a 'complicated' recipe for a special occasion than it is to whip up something like a sandwich for lunch every day. I use saved recipes when I cook from scratch, no matter how basic the dish or how many times I've made it before.

Going food shopping with a list

I know 'just make a list' might sound like the most useless tip in existence but it really works here. Even when I was a 22-year-old junior journalist, I used meal planners and shopping lists like a middle-aged mum of three, and didn't care if rugby lad housemates laughed at me for being too organized. It saves me impulse-buying food and leaving vegetables to rot. What's not to like?

Making foods where flavour matters more than presentation

When chefs on cookery programmes talk about their favourite food, or the food they remember from childhood, they don't usually talk about fiddly, fancy-pants Michelin starred cuisine; they talk about fish and chips at the seaside, or their grandma's throw-everything-into-the-pot family favourite. When people describe someone as a good cook, they aren't usually referring to how magnificently fast they can chop vegetables. Ultimately, food is meant to taste good more than look pretty. Rice and pasta dishes are great examples of this and easy to bulk or batch cook.

Timing everything
All phones and most kitchen gadgets have timers on them. I use them for everything, from bread baking to leaving packet noodles to stand for one minute.

Having a plan B when cooking for others
I always try to have a backup plan when I'm cooking for anyone else. This could be ordering a takeaway, or having a ready meal I can quickly serve up instead in case of disaster.

Owning the best kitchen implements I possibly can
After being a professional chef or a serial murderer, being dyspraxic is probably the third most-likely thing that can make you ask for a good quality kitchen knife for Christmas. Although the most expensive knives are often the sharpest, they're also easier to cut with so you're less likely to injure yourself overall.

Watching other people preparing and talking about food
Although my mum wasn't patient enough to actually teach me many skills, she learned how to cook well from my grandma, and, through not growing up with money, knew how to make something from nothing. Watching her cook and talking about cooking with her as an adult have gradually helped me find cooking easier. If there's someone in your life who can teach you to peel carrots without a civil war breaking out, all the better. If you have children, involving them in food preparation in simple ways according to what they can manage is recognized as a good way

to help them build a happy relationship with food. A dyspraxic mum-of-three I know told me how she manages mealtimes by giving each of the children a different job in the kitchen: brilliant fun for them and brilliantly stress-saving for her.

Read on for more about eating and cooking with others…

Dyspraxic dreads: Eating, drinking and cooking in groups

In decades past, going out to eat was much more of a rare treat for anybody, and eating or drinking in public spaces was frowned on. My teens and twenties coincided with the rise of 24-hour drinking, fast food and workplace socializing, which meant a lot of group eating and drinking. Though social media and online events now make this easier to avoid if you prefer to, you might recognize some of the situations outlined below.

Making tea or carrying drinks for lots of people

The mistake I made with tea rounds was thinking it would be more polite to say yes to a cup of tea occasionally than to keep saying 'No thanks' just to avoid having to carry six full cups across an office. If you accept tea or a drink from people, they'll usually expect you to return the gesture and possibly get shirty with you if you don't. To make things easier, it's best just to offer drinks to the person nearest you rather than a whole group, or just make or order drinks for yourself whenever you want them. If you really can't get out of massive tea or drinks rounds, use a carrier rather than a tray, carry two at a time, and save everyone's tea preferences as a note on your phone.

Struggling with chopsticks

Stimulant medication has helped my dyspraxia enough that I've learned to use chopsticks. Before that, I always asked for a knife and fork instead, and there's absolutely nothing wrong with this. Anyone who eats with chopsticks will understand that it's difficult if you're not used to them, and you're far more likely to attract negative attention by trying to struggle through it than just quietly doing what works.

Events with no space to sit down to eat
I still remember the birthday party from my childhood where another girl had a go at me for moving someone's things off a chair so I could sit there while I was eating. Stand-up events are a neurodivergent nemesis. I always look for somewhere to sit down while I eat, even if it means breaking away from a group.

Struggling to find somewhere to eat
There's nothing worse than wandering around looking for food in a place you don't know (or thought you knew, but it turns out, you don't remember as well as you thought…), especially if you don't have a car and have been walking for hours. Although online booking and restaurant guides have made this very preventable, the internet can't help you if you wrongly assume everywhere will be open or have space for you. Hard lessons learned in my life: snacky places are often too rammed or close early on big occasions like New Year's Eve, and restaurants often aren't open early in the week or on Sundays.

Cooking for guests
Thanks to glossy TV shows and adverts, lots of us grow up with the idea that being able to host dinner parties is some essential part of adulthood, rather than something that's actually hard for a lot of people for a lot of reasons. It's perfectly possible to have friends or a loving extended family and never in your life want to invite several of them at a time around for a meal. Paying for a

meal, ordering a takeaway and buying a ready meal or a nice box of chocolates is just as much a way to show your appreciation for someone with food than cooking for them. If you feel confident enough to contemplate cooking for guests, my number one tip is to cook something you can prepare in advance and heat up when they arrive, or suggest a sharing plates dinner where everyone brings something for the meal. Or if you're lucky enough to have space at home, make a side dish and get more confident cooks to prepare the main in your kitchen.

Events or trips which involve preparing food as a group
This can include certain types of holidays, birthday parties and stag and hen dos. And frankly, I just flatly avoid them – and team activity holidays in general – unless I feel clear enough about what's involved and comfortable enough telling people what I can and can't do.

Surprise celebrations involving the above
'This isn't anything that's going to make me look silly, is it?' I once asked one of my best friends nervously when we arrived for a birthday surprise.

'You know I'd never do that to you,' she replied, and we had a lovely day.

If you're worried about someone arranging a surprise, there are nice ways of letting people know what kind of celebrations you prefer or prefer to avoid before they have a chance to arrange anything.

Neurodivergence, drink and drugs

If you're neurodivergent, the idea of taking something that affects your brain and body in uncertain ways can either seem like a great reason to spend your life drunk or high or to avoid doing so. For me as a dyspraxic woman, the more off-putting thing about smoking or drugs than death and disease was probably the idea of learning how to do something with my hands in front of others. As a young budding journalist in the days when indoor smoking was still legal, I bought or 'looked after' packets of cigarettes to attempt to learn to smoke by myself and even practised asking for them over the counter so I sounded confident and blasé enough. Some years later, my boss at the time offered me one of his, then laughed and immediately snatched it back like I was a toddler making a mess with my dinner. That public humiliation was enough to ensure I never smoked again.

The mess I made of cutting up my ADHD pills to get the right dose during titration, then trying to line up the powder with my Runners Need store card, similarly confirmed I was an unlikely candidate for a coke habit. Knowing that I'm emotionally wobbly and anything I liked tended to consume my life, going near addictive substances just never really felt a good plan.

However, for someone with no addiction issues, an inordinate number of people I was close to in my twenties were either recovering addicts or had parents or partners who were, which pointed to something and suggested my stance on drugs also had a lot to do with luck that I had met them all in recovery and not before. If any of my favourite people at the time had regularly offered me powder or pills to loosen me up, I'm not sure my self-awareness or dyspraxic fear of doing it wrong would have put me off joining in for long. My mum told me one of her greatest reliefs as a parent was that I was a sensible drinker who could stop after one or two at dinner and not carry on until I was wasted. When my ADHD doctor mentioned the relationship between neurodivergence and addiction, I felt relieved myself, and some of the most significant relationships and encounters of my twenties made sense.

ADHD and addiction

People can become addicted to substances for all sorts of reasons which aren't for me to unpack. But as I've touched on already in previous chapters, one of the main reasons why ADHDers in particular are thought to be more vulnerable to addiction than the general population is because street drugs and alcohol are the most easily available way to give our brains the dopamine we use up too fast. Some addiction counsellors have a very broad definition of addiction and say that all types of addiction are essentially the same whether they're chemical or psychological. Other people I've spoken to and heard from over the years – both those with dependency histories and medical professionals – disagree. A close friend and recovering alcoholic dismissed me when I described myself as addicted to chocolate, or to a person: 'Max, you've never stolen from your own family to buy chocolate or go and see someone!' he harrumphed. Other times, though, he pointed out similarities between my obsessive behaviour and that of a problem drinker or drug user. The bottom line is that booze and recreational drugs, unlike people or things, are highly physically addictive, so safe withdrawal is really important. There are links to support with drugs and alcohol at the end of the book. There's more about obsessive relationships in the next chapter.

Neurodivergence and sleep

I've met people who go against stereotypes of neurodivergence in all kinds of ways. I've even met a dyspraxic man who found driving easy. But without exception, every single neurodivergent person I've ever met and spoken to about it has suffered from insomnia for as long as they can remember. If your parents still talk about how you never slept when you were a child even though you're old enough to be a parent yourself, or you've learned to hide the timestamps on your messages so people don't worry about you, you're not alone.

Although nobody knows why, it's thought that we're more likely to experience something called delayed sleep phase syndrome. This means our natural circadian rhythm, which controls when we feel tired, is delayed, so we feel tired later than most people and wake up later than most people.

There are other reasons why it might be difficult to sleep. We might tend to hyperfocus on tasks we can't tear ourselves away from, which stops us going to bed or switching off. We might be kept awake by racing thoughts. We might also process thoughts and feelings more slowly, so they're more likely to catch up with us at the end of the day.

So what can we do about it? Unfortunately, the number one sleep hygiene tip about only using your bedroom for sleep is true, but not much use if you only have one room to use for everything. The same goes for sleeping somewhere different from usual. I was once referred to a free sleep clinic where two men compared which Caribbean islands were best for holidays. If I could have afforded that for a change of scene, I'm sure I'd have slept better.

Some people swear by keeping their phone out of their room or locking themselves out of certain phone apps, but I find these things punitive, and although I do block certain sites on my computer, I haven't found one that works for the apps on my phone. Some people deal with the bedtime rush of thoughts by keeping a pen and paper by the bed to jot down any stray thoughts. Or, if you can use your phone's Notes function without ending up on an online shopping spree or down a Google rabbit hole, do that instead.

ADHD medication helps some people get to sleep and rein in their phone usage before bed, but it can also lead to sleep problems. My doctor recommends taking your medication before 9am so it's out of your body by bedtime, and drinking orange juice before you go to bed to decrease the effects, so you feel tired rather than energetic.

> **The five sleeping tips in the world that work for me**
>
> 1. **Being out of the house at least once a day for something other than work.** On a good day, this means going for a long walk or a run. On a less good day, this is just going for a five-minute walk around the block, or sticking my head out of the back door for a few minutes.
> 2. **Having a goal of when to get to sleep during the week**, and sticking as closely to it as possible. I use the iPhone's winddown function as a signal to start thinking of bedtime, but there are days I feel super tired and go to bed earlier, or shrug it off when I'm feeling wide awake.
> 3. **Having a daily bedtime ritual.** I listen to a short daily radio programme or a longer podcast. Even if I get absorbed in a long podcast for a few more minutes than I want to, it eventually helps me drift off. If you work in your bedroom, you could create the feeling of a separate space by putting a cloth over your desk/laptop, or stashing your laptop out of sight.
> 4. **Taking my medication at the same time every morning.** This gives me something to get out of bed for every day, whatever else I'm doing or not doing.
> 5. **Knowing what makes my sleep worse.** For much

> of my life, I barely even knew what a good night's sleep was. Nowadays, I sleep well or badly in waves, and knowing this helps me to be kinder to myself about it. Certain things universally affect sleep, especially difficult and unexpected news. One November, after finding out a particular type of difficult news unexpectedly for the third time in my life, I spent several days and nights hyperfocused on looking up unaffordable tropical holidays, then scaled down my plans to a more modest night out with friends and a back massage, and fell back into a better sleep routine with it.
>
> Other things that can affect sleep are alcohol, being premenstrual and eating heavy meals before going to bed.

Neurodivergence and exercise (or 'Yes, I found some I actually enjoyed...')

Nothing would astonish my younger self more than how I've turned into someone who actually chooses to exercise and enjoys it. After the legally enforced torture that was PE as an undiagnosed dyspraxic. I'll never be the sort of person who wants to impose my hobbies on other people. But I strongly believe that if you're dyspraxic there is a way of moving your body you can enjoy if you're given the right chance to find it. At the age of 30, I went from someone who could barely run to catch a train to a long-distance runner in a year. I ran the London Marathon, which even my very dextrous partner who will happily camp for four days without wi-fi hasn't seen the need to put himself through yet. What follows is my advice for a happier relationship with exercise.

Know why it helps

We've all heard that exercise in general is good for us. But for ADHDers there's a very specific reason why, as it's one of the big producers of the dopamine we get through too quickly. Although it's not as efficient as the dopamine you get through medication, it can help medication work, and also help compensate for the days when medication is less effective because of your hormones. ADHDers without dyspraxia are stereotypically drawn to sporty activities as a way of managing their ADHD. Dyspraxic ADHDers are less likely to be, so we can face the double disadvantage of struggling with something in one way that would actually help us in another.

Have a deeply personal reason to do it

My exercise journey began when I was broken by grief too complicated to express in words and needed a reason to leave the house. Obviously, I don't wish this particular reason on anybody. But if you're dyspraxic, having an emotional reason to do something practical or physical can often, literally, be what moves you.

Start solo, simple and cheap

If your experience of exercise up until now involves cringing at the back of a smelly, crowded gym and trying not to be noticed, small-group or solo exercise is most probably for you. Apps such as *Couch to 5K* come with built-in training plans that are designed to help beginners stick to them. I still use *Couch to 5K* when I'm returning to running after a break. If you feel you want to join a class, there are an increasing number of disability-friendly classes around. Some years ago, despite stretching the definition of 'youth', I joined a ballet class run by youth group Dyspraxic Me, which is the only place I'd ever want to experience ballet. I was once the only one who turned up, new, to a spin class because the regulars had all mistakenly been sent the wrong date, and treated the gently baffled instructor to an emotional speech about dyspraxia. For some years, I did a small-group Pilates class: whatever your feelings about being 'out' as a dyspraxic person, it's often useful for exercise instructors to know.

Find different exercises to suit different energy levels

I once trained for a half marathon and did a dress rehearsal run of the full distance on day two of my period, which, funnily enough, I don't highly recommend. When I'm busy writing, I try to manage half an hour of running or (mostly pavement or off-road) cycling one to three times a week. When I'm busy writing and hormonal and it's November, my goal shifts to fitting in a daily walk around the block while it's still daylight.

Neurodivergence and your cycle (hormones, not bikes...)

Periods are no fun for anyone who has them. But if you're neurodivergent, having the monthly ritual of pains and stains thrown into your life is even less inviting.

Period products

I use a Mooncup because I don't have to remember to buy it and the expense helps me guard against losing it, which has only happened once in a decade, just after I moved house. I also keep some spare pads at home in case, and if visitors need them. If you're worried about dropping your Mooncup down the loo, you could empty it into the sink. But some sinks block if you do this, so use a bucket of water or bowl if you're not sure. If neither of these is an option, I tend to wipe it as clean as I can with loo roll until I'm somewhere I can clean it better, or leave it in until I get home.

Avoiding the dreaded jam stain

Long dark clothes have been a lifesaver for me, as has period underwear. They aren't cheap, but one or two pairs can see you through the heaviest days of a period. They're also great if your flow is unpredictable. Clean them with water and stick them in your normal wash. Don't use heaps of extra detergent or softener because this wears down the fabric and makes them less effective.

Cleaning up

It can be mortifying to leave traces of blood behind you without noticing, and bits of blood have a way of clinging to everything and making you wonder how they got there. The most common places are the toilet (bowl, seat and rim), the sink, the floor around the toilet, and the loo roll. However, it's easy to forget to check, or miss it. If you're really paranoid, you could keep a small bottle of sanitizer or travel shampoo in your handbag.

Tracking periods

You probably already use a period tracker app. As well as when my period is due, I use it to log a couple of other symptoms throughout the month, which helps me remember to look at it. If you struggle with PMS, it's a good idea to set it to remind you of when you're in your PMS phase. Some years, I've used a paper diary which stays on my desk and I've attached a sticky note to the pages to remind me I have PMS, which I shift to the following month. Also, as you get a bit older, period trackers can help you see when your cycle starts to change and the gaps between your periods get more erratic, then longer, or your periods change.

Pain relief
Either keep it in one place and have a routine of taking it, or keep stashes in different places where you're likely to need it. It's especially handy to keep some by the bed in case you wake up in pain.

Things that affect your cycle you might not have been told about
These can include stress, travelling, the time of year and (a new one on most people) heavy exercise. They can affect your flow and how long your periods last, as well as when you come on.

Smear tests

The strange thing about my dyspraxic life is that my most awkward and painful experiences have never been the ones you might think of as being awkward. My first smear test rates alongside vaccinations and having my ears pierced as my most unexpectedly pain-free and cringe-free experiences. However, I know too many women who put up with unnecessary pain and horrible treatment. I'll assume you know why smear tests are important and I'll cut straight to the neurodivergent survival guide.

Where and when to go for a smear
In the UK, you'll usually get an NHS letter inviting you. The age of your first invite or how often you're invited may be different depending on whereabouts you live. You should still go for a smear even if you don't have sex with men, or at all. The test will probably be done by a woman; if not, you can request this.

In some areas, you can choose to do the test yourself at home, which some neurodivergent and disabled women I know find helpful. If you have periods, try to go in the middle of your cycle. This is usually when your body is naturally lubricated.

What to wear to a smear
Try to wear a skirt instead of trousers, if you can. It's not the end of the world if you forget, but it makes it easier.

Pain fears (and myths about pain)
If you're worried because it's your first smear or you've had bad experiences with smears in the past, you can say you're nervous or ask for more lube or a smaller speculum, without giving a reason. How sexually experienced you are, what kind of sex you have or how sensitive you are to other types of pain won't necessarily affect whether a smear is painful or not.

What happens during a smear
You'll probably be shown into a room with a bed behind a screen or curtain, then asked to take off your pants and lie down. They might ask you to clench your fists slightly and place them just under your bum. This is to lift you up and make it easier for them to get in and do what they need to, especially if you have a tilted (or 'shy') cervix, which most people who do aren't aware of. A nurse once praised me for doing it without prompting, which is possibly the strangest praise I've ever had. Don't worry if you forget or if they don't prompt you straight away – if they need you to, they'll let you know.

Other questions to expect
Whoever does your test will probably ask when your last period was, whether there's any chance you might be pregnant and whether you've given birth recently. They might ask if you've

had any problems with smears in the past, whether this is your first smear, or if you have any history of health conditions like sexually transmitted infections (STIs). They may also ask if you're 'sexually active'. If you're wondering what counts as sex, see 'Neurodivergence and your sex life' in Chapter 11. You shouldn't be asked anything else directly about your sex life or history and you don't have to tell them anything else unless you want to.

Small talk
While they do the test, they'll probably try to put you at ease with small talk, like asking you what you do for work. I was once asked by a lovely nurse to give a synopsis of a book I was writing. I joked she was the most interested in my book of anybody who'd ever seen me with my pants down.

If small talk is difficult for you, you have the right to mention before your appointment that you're neurodivergent and would prefer not to chat. Or if there's something particular you prefer to talk about, such as one of your strong interests, that would help calm you down, you could let them know.

If you're not sure what counts as a socially acceptable subject and don't want to risk a negative reaction, ask a trusted neurotypical or someone more confident with neurotypical social norms. Subjects like food, hair, makeup, beauty products and travel (unless your travel plans involve something wildly off the beaten track like going to a South American death festival...) are usually safe.

How to look good as a neurodivergent person (You don't need heels...)

Social media has opened up the world of fashion and beauty to a more diverse selection of influencers, beauty vloggers and writers than ever before. I would have loved to have grown up in today's world, where there are disabled and chronically ill women creating fashion and beauty tutorials, instead of one where there was no alternative to the narrow and punishing beauty regimes of people with endless time, money and, most of all, dexterity. Here are my dyspraxic and ADHD-friendly tips on everything to do with how you look.

Know your best and your bare minimum days
Everyone's idea of what it means to look their best is different, and no one looks their best all the time. As with everything else, accepting your best and worst days is key to life as a neurodivergent person. My 'best' days involve being able to apply full eyeshadow. My 'bare minimum' days, usually around my period, involve being able to shower and get dressed at some point during the day. For some people, a bad day might mean that showering or brushing your teeth is difficult because of sensory issues. If this is you, keeping a 'bad day' supply of wet wipes or chewable toothpaste can be handy.

Flaunting looks you find easiest to create yourself
As much as I admired my well-coordinated friend's ability to do eyeliner, I learned that a better use of my time was to make the most of the looks I could easily do on my own. Some years ago, I was given a set of professional makeup brushes, including a lip brush. The long brush made it easier for me to apply lipstick. Now, bright lipstick is my 'thing'. I'm rarely without it and I'm building up a collection.

Asking for looks you can't do or afford to have done yourself as a treat or a skill swap
Shoes and coats are often worth spending more on as you might be more heavy-footed or spend more time outside and on your

feet if you don't drive. Again, I sometimes ask for them as presents or buy them from charity shops or thrift stores in expensive areas. For dyspraxics who want to remove body hair, the best razor or hair removal cream you can afford is a good buy. As with kitchen equipment, buying a super-sharp non-disposable razor might sound like a bad idea, but the quality also means you're less likely to hurt yourself with it. My wonderful easy-grip razor was made by an eco-friendly company that send refills every three months. I also have an electric flosser which my dentist recommends to dyspraxic patients: another Christmas present.

Knowing what's worth spending more on and what you can buy cheaply

Shoes and coats are often worth spending more on as you might be more heavy-footed or spend more time outside and on your feet if you don't drive. Again, I sometimes ask for them as presents or buy them from charity shops or thrift stores in expensive areas. For dyspraxics who want to remove body hair, as I said above, the best razor or hair removal cream you can afford is a good buy.

Keeping certain clothes for work or going out

I try to keep some clothes specifically for work, going out or when I need to look presentable on camera, so they're not dirty when I need them.

Using a packing list and a leaving routine for 'important' occasions

I use the mantra 'Purse, phone, keys' to make sure I never leave home without them. My partner and I do this when we leave the house together. If I need to leave the house with anything else, I use a tick list on my phone to pack.

Encouraging people not to distract you while you're getting ready

People who aren't aware you struggle with memory tend to well-meaningly overload you with suggestions that will lead to you forgetting and losing things. For example, 'Why don't you wear your other coat instead? It looks really nice!', which means you swap coats and leave something important in the pocket of the other coat.

Keeping jewellery on

Jewellery stays on me until the end of the day and only comes off in a dedicated part of my bedroom or whatever room I'm sleeping in. If someone buys you a nice piece of jewellery and well-meaningly suggests you should take it off every time you wash your hands/wash up/breathe, either respectfully ignore them or ask them if you can swap it for something else that can be left on. The chances of you leaving it next to a public sink and never seeing it again are much greater than the risk of any damage.

Wearing the prettiest flat shoes you can find

There's an old German saying that translates as 'If you want to look good, you must suffer', which I'm pretty sure was coined by someone who's watched a dyspraxic person try to walk in high heel shoes. One of the first and last times I wore heels in public was to a job interview, where, fortunately, I managed to save tripping over for the street outside afterwards.

On another occasion, a random drunk man started singing the old song 'Lady in Red', and adding 'who walks like a penguin'. There are whole shops devoted to ballet pumps of many shapes and colours. Shoes really don't have to be high to be pretty. If you're desperate to wear heels, the chunky kind are easier than the stiletto kind.

Ignoring rubbish about ageing

Contrary to what certain sections of the media insist, being past 35 does not mean you're basically dead. As a student, I mainly lived in band hoodies except for a couple of formal events a term, and sighed at girls who spent hours perfecting their makeup and donning sequinned boob tubes just to go for a couple of drinks at the pub. In my thirties, heavy makeup and designer shades became my armour against everything the previous 10–15 years had thrown at me. At my best friend's wedding recently, I was with a group of schoolfriends who similarly lived in band hoodies when we were younger. We all looked so glam we could've been promoting a glossy Netflix series.

Another joy of getting older is less street harassment. Lowlights of my twenties range from the unprintable to being asked whether a blind celebrity had cut my hair. These days, I'm much more likely to be stopped in the street by other women asking where I got my clothes from.

Neurodivergent body behaviours that don't go in cute memes...

Tearing your hair out (or picking your nose...)

A while ago, in the run up to moving house, I started tearing my hair out in the evenings. No, literally. And not just the hair on my head. My downstairs looked like a piece of children's art made out of an old Brillo pad. I also developed a strange urge to clear my throat all the time while at my desk and had random coughing fits in public – particularly inconvenient given there had just been a global pandemic. These things are examples of body-focused repetitive behaviours (BFRBs), sometimes also called tics and stims. Others include picking your skin, scalp or nose. Most BFRBs aren't harmful, and unless you can't control where you do them, you're unlikely to need treatment. But talking about them can be hard, as can the fear of accidentally doing them where you can be seen. As is often recommended, I tried using a fidget toy to replace the behaviour. Unfortunately, my invitingly squidgy stress ball only lasted three days before my fingernail pierced a hole in it and covered my desk and bedroom in purple slime. As with hypersexuality (below), stimulant medication can help BFRBs or bring them on in different people or at different times.

Medication giving you the raging horn

I used to laugh sardonically at people who said stimulants made them hypersexual, when what they made me want to do was mainly be able to just sit down at my desk unsupervised and without crying. Then one day several months into taking them, an unsexy scene in a largely unsexy novel I was writing suddenly and inexplicably turned into a porn fest. Another week, I lost a morning or two to pretty elaborate fantasies about people I'd never remotely fancied before in my life. If this happens to you and lasts for more than a few days, tell your prescriber that it's affecting your life. If and when (and only then...) it feels as if you have lasting chemistry with someone that it would genuinely be a good idea to act on, think about letting them know. Otherwise, just let it be quietly there until it passes.

Forgetting to get washed, dressed or go to the loo

Hyperfocus can make you so engrossed you forget to do everything else, including, well, the one thing we all do. This can lead to constipation or the opposite. The best solutions are to work as close to a loo as you can and find somewhere discreet to clean and dry your clothes. Another common situation is ending up going out and forgetting to wash your hair. Dry shampoo and keeping body spray in all your going out bags can help.

Leaving unintended messes behind you

One day aged about 12 when I was visiting my grandparents, I forgot to pick up my clothes from the bathroom floor and overheard them having a disagreement about whether to get me out of bed to pick them up. I could hear they were bewildered as to how their well-behaved granddaughter who'd grown up in a tidy house could think it was okay to just step out of her clothes into the bath and leave them there. I hated going to stay there for years after that and told nobody the truth about why. A lot later, I realized that little incidents like these were linked to my attention and memory problems. You're especially likely to forget to clean up after yourself when you're out of routine and visiting someone else's home. In this case, a simple apology will probably do. If you live with other people, explaining could literally be a marriage-saver.

Serious accidents

Dyspraxia and/or ADHD can lead to accidents which can be anything from expensively damaging (wearing out the carpet from pacing, or accidentally flooding the bathroom) to literally dangerous (there have been cases of people's houses burning down around them while hyperfocusing (Flippin, 2024), and kitchen fires due to dyspraxic accidents).

If you regularly have accidents this serious, you should be eligible for support. This might be extra payments to help with costs of living with a disability (currently known as a Personal Independence Payment or PIP in the UK), a support worker, or both. I'm not an expert on what's available in every area or country and you should speak to someone who is. In the UK or Australia, Citizens Advice can help with this. Self-advocacy groups set up for disabled and/or neurodivergent people can too. There are some listed at the end of the book.

Neurodivergence and weather

For various reasons, being neurodivergent can make very hot or very cold weather particularly difficult to manage. This can include sensory issues, increased clumsiness (who hasn't dropped their phone on a hot or cold day?) and finding it harder to cope with weather extremes or changing weather. The country where I'm from and live isn't known for being particularly hot or cold, and people here, whatever their neurotype, tend to erupt with a mixture of excitement or panic if the temperature goes above or below 20 degrees.

In the UK, there are two ways ADHDers tend to react to weather: some of us overcompensate for planning difficulties by obsessively over-packing, layering and app-checking to allow for every possible climate: 'You're in England. How are you not prepared for rain?' one friend says to anyone who gets caught out by a shower. My mum is also an obsessive planner and who will insist everyone leaves the house with more changes of clothes than an army platoon in case they get too hot or too cold for a few minutes. Alternatively, some of us just wear whatever we want to, regardless of the weather (hello former boyfriend who wore shorts and open sandals in London in November...).

These are my top three weather tips for neurodivergent people not used to extreme weather:

1. **Learn about weather extremes from the people who live with them all the time:** Half my family is from an East German mountain village and I've shared a house with an Australian, so I could fill a whole book with cold and hot weather advice. They're the people to ask, and are usually on hand to give advice when British social media goes bananas during a heatwave or a cold snap.

2. **Don't expect to move around much or get anywhere fast:** It's hard to be productive if you aren't used to it, and in the UK, unusual weather tends to make things break. If you're going to a place where the extreme weather isn't temporary, see the above tip.

3. **Use a daily face moisturizer with built-in sun protection all year round:** Every year without fail, the first hot day of the year catches me by surprise and burns me to a crisp, especially since I've moved to the seaside. A tip I once learned from an Australian housemate is to use a daily face moisturizer with built-in sun protection all year round. This stops my face looking like a tangerine on the first day of summer. The sky's the limit when it comes to how much you can spend on skincare, but you can pick up a perfectly decent one pretty cheaply. Light travel perfume is also a good idea if your senses can tolerate it.

Buy 'going out' clothes you can adapt to seasons

An example of this is long skirts that you can wear with or without tights. This makes life easier during the transition seasons (autumn and spring) when the weather is especially unreliable. While writing this book, I came across some intriguing research from Australia which suggests that rates of ADHD are lower and traits easier to manage in hot countries because warm weather is a source of dopamine (Science Daily, 2013). Given that most people in Britain with or without ADHD would say they're happier and more motivated when the sun shines, this seems difficult to measure, and is disputed (Children and Adults with Attention-Deficit/Hyperactivity Disorder, 2018). But it might explain why major research into ADHD and dyspraxia tends to happen in cold parts of the world like Scandinavia (Gillberg, 2024) and

Canada (CanChild, n.d.). If you need a reason to move somewhere hot, this might be it...

Final thoughts

Staying with the theme of mess, quite simply the best stain remover in the world is cheap shampoo. It lasts well, and you can buy it everywhere.

The next chapter is all about driving and is for neurodivergent people who are learners, new drivers, non-drivers or undecided about whether to learn.

CHAPTER 9: A QUICK RECAP

- You don't have to love your body. You can learn to like it. And you have as much right to eat, have sex and look good as anyone else.
- Your hormones can affect your neurodivergence. Managing your life around your monthly cycle can make life easier.
- Certain non-cute bodily habits can be ways of relieving stress. They probably don't need treatment unless they harm you or anyone else.

CHAPTER 10

Getting Around and Driving

Or 'How Do I Make Getting Around
Easier? Will I Ever Learn to Drive?'

This chapter is about getting where you need to go – literally. Originally, I made it all about my number one neurodivergent nemesis: learning to drive. Plenty of neurodivergent people can and do drive, and own a car. But for many of us, learning to drive takes a lot of time, practice and patience. We're more likely to learn later in life, not want to at all, or not be able to because of co-occurring disabilities or health conditions.

Dyspraxia makes driving especially challenging, and as it's so under-recognized, many people try to learn without knowing they are. And although my dyspraxia diagnosis came before ADHD, it's more common for adults with other types of neurodivergence not to recognize dyspraxia in themselves.

As someone who eventually passed a driving test in my thirties, I know plenty about the pros, cons, highs and lows of life as both a driver and a passenger. So rather than just aiming this chapter at learner drivers, I've divided it into two sections: first,

'Life without driving', and second, 'A neurodivergent's guide to driving'.

Life without driving

Let's start with the biggest pros of not driving. Thanks to online shopping and remote working, living and getting around as a non-driver is easier now than it's been at any time since cars were invented. If you live in or close to a major city and don't need to go anywhere else, public transport is often more convenient, cheaper and, of course, greener. These reasons are often part of the decision to learn late or not at all.

Being invited to things you can't get to because you don't drive

Middle-of-nowhere events organized on the assumption that everyone will be driving are every non-driver's least favourite thing. If someone expects you to be somewhere you can't get to easily, it's perfectly okay to let them know and expect them to care. If you're the one arranging to see someone, then it's more on you to figure out how to get to them before you invite them, but if they're worth getting to, they should still want you to make it as easy for yourself as possible.

Arranging lifts with other people

I've heard drivers complain about non-drivers always wanting lifts, when actually, most in my experience are happier to sit on a train. If someone giving you a lift means they have to wait for you or it makes their journey longer, it's polite to give them a small gift or some money towards petrol. If that's not affordable, offer them a favour in return. But if they're dropping you home on the way to and from somewhere, especially if it's a one-off, then that's a bit excessive.

The thing I've learned about asking for lifts from other people is that it's always best to check with the person driving yourself rather than rely on someone else telling you it's okay. There's nothing worse than being assured, 'So-and-so can pick you up!', then finding out on the day that so-and-so is in a mood with you because she didn't know she was meant to be giving you a lift and you couldn't be bothered to ask her yourself. If you don't have the driver's number to check, weigh up the risk against the faff of making other arrangements, or how important the event is. If you need to be somewhere regularly, or at short notice, and don't want to keep asking the same friends or family, organized carpools or community groups are good places to find lifts without social drama.

If someone resents giving you a lift and does it anyway, that's their problem. But one way to avoid resentment is to genuinely want to be there yourself. Something else I learned in my peak going-out years is not to force myself to go to events I can't easily get to on my own and also know I'm unlikely to enjoy.

Walking *everywhere* because you don't drive

I used to joke that having to walk everywhere rather than drive was dyspraxia's way of making up for all the other exercise I didn't do. I'm so used to it, I forget that some people who are used to driving see a person wandering the streets alone and assume something terrible has happened to them, hence the number of times drivers have stopped to ask me whether I'm okay or need a lift.

Public transport as a non-driver

Some of my happiest and saddest memories in life involve train and bus journeys. I've travelled all over the UK on public transport, meeting sometimes lovely and sometimes not-so-lovely people on the way. In my younger years especially, I was especially prone to letting people make me feel stupid for not knowing something when there was actually no reason why I should have done or the information was easy to miss, and public transport is one place where this tends to happen. If I'm confused about something despite someone's best efforts to help and explain, I'm always grateful, polite and apologetic. If, however, someone gets grumpy, I say calmly, 'I appreciate you do this every day, but I don't.'

If you're not someone who gets excited by trains or planes, it might seem like an annoying neurodivergent stereotype, but train and plane geeks are great people to know when it comes to sniffing out well-hidden bargains or collecting important bits of information to make your journey run smoothly. If you rely on public transport, getting to know the big ones on social media could save you a lot of money and time.

Electronic rather than paper tickets make it harder to forget or lose your ticket on public transport, but much easier to order the wrong one by mistake, especially if you're in a hurry. I know several neurodivergent people who've successfully challenged transport fines under the Equality Act.

Back in Chapter 4, I mentioned sunflower lanyards, and public transport is a situation where they can be most helpful. I carry one, which is clipped to the inside of my travel bag.

Looking for work when you don't drive

The rise of remote working and car-free incentives has made life for some disabled and neurodivergent people easier in many ways, especially when it comes to one of the worst types of indirect discrimination at work: needing to drive in order to get there. Starting my career before my diagnosis and before video calling was mainstream limited me to work within walking distance, even if it involved four weeks of stuffing envelopes at a tobacco company. People who worried about my work prospects for a multitude of other reasons never seemed to consider that not being able to drive or not having a car might have been my greatest employment barrier of all. I was still far luckier than some. Early in my journalism career, I came across a dyspraxic mother who didn't drive and had been forced to live away from her son in order to find work in an area where she didn't need a car to do it.

Sadly, charities and other organizations that represent neurodivergent people have been more timid than other disability groups at standing up for non-drivers on this issue. While it's understandable that they don't want to imply that neurodivergent people are unsafe drivers and upset those of us who've been driving safely for years, this isn't a reason to throw non-drivers under the bus, as it were.

So where do you stand when you see the dreaded 'full driving licence required' on a job advert?

The Equality Act says that driving should only be essential for work if 1) it's directly related to the job, such as a delivery driver, or 2) the travelling you need to do for work isn't possible by public transport. In the UK, Access to Work should also pay for you to get to work by taxi if because of a disability it isn't possible for you to get there another way.

One final, vital point is that job descriptions often say you need to be able to drive simply because they've been copied and pasted across from somewhere else, so it's always worth challenging. And if a recruiter says anything judgemental about you not driving, *definitely* challenge them with great force...

Being questioned or judged by other people for not driving
I once saw someone in recruitment state publicly that they looked down on candidates who hadn't learned to drive,

believing it to be a sign of laziness. Anyone in recruitment who does this needs to know they're breaking the Equality Act.

Strangely, taxi drivers have often taken the keenest interest in me not driving, which seems a bit career-limiting of them. I've never asked anyone who hires me because they struggle with writing why they can't spell. If you want to explain without getting into a much longer conversation, try:

- 'I'm tired.'
- 'I'm drinking.'
- 'I really like travelling by train/bus.'
- 'My car is in for a service.'

You could also abruptly change the subject ('Oh look, there's that new Chinese takeaway! Have you been?') or say you need to look at something urgent on your phone.

Another reason people can get strange around you for not driving is if it makes them think you're an alcoholic or a drug user. I've found that saying 'Long story...' and laughing nervously when people ask why you don't drive tends to unintentionally imply these things to people. Or indeed, you might actually be one. Even if their reaction is totally understandable, for example if they lost their child to drugs or in a drink-driving accident, their judgement is their issue, not yours.

Something that's more common than outright judgement or criticism is people who are just forgetful or puzzled about how long it takes or how hard it is for you to learn to drive, or who assume you'll be able to learn quickly when you need to. My dyslexic, dexterous partner learned quickly at an early age, then moved to London and just hired a car occasionally to get to out-of-the-way places. His driving test probably ranks alongside ordering a ropey kebab in terms of its significance to his life. I explained to him that learning to drive and ensuring that I'm a safe driver has taken up roughly the same energy as a second job, only I paid for it.

Being more vulnerable in relationships because you don't drive

One of the top signs of abuse in relationships is when the victim is physically isolated. Of course, a driver going out with someone who doesn't drive doesn't make them an abuser. But in some areas, being without a car is unfortunately one of the easiest ways for your partner or someone you live with to make you dependent on them if they want to. Even in relationships that weren't abusive, not driving has made me feel dependent on others to an unhealthy degree. One of my biggest reasons for not getting into a particular relationship when I was younger was because it would have meant moving to a strange place in the middle of nowhere without anybody else I knew around me and no certainty of ever being able to drive. Though I wasn't always sensible in my twenties, I'm immensely relieved and proud of myself for recognizing what a deeply unhappy and even dangerous situation that would have been.

If you don't drive because of a disability, or for any reason, you're also entitled to want to live in a place where you can get around independently wherever possible and not just be expected to rely on someone else to get further than your front door.

Being asked for directions by drivers (or other unanswerable questions about cars, and traffic moans...)

Sat navs and smartphones have happily reduced the need for something many older dyspraxics used to dread. If you've never had the experience of someone yelling 'LEFT OR RIGHT? *LEFT OR RIGHT??!!*' at you from behind the wheel in terror, you're not missing anything. But some people still mistrust sat navs or can't be bothered to enter postcodes and so insist on taking directions from you instead, especially if they're driving you home. 'Why can't you tell me the way to your own house?' a nasty taxi driver once said to my dyspraxic friend, making her cry.

If you're unlucky enough to meet someone like this, try not to let them make you feel apologetic and just be as firm as you can. A good reply to the above would have been: 'People often get confused by my directions and it's led to a few hairy moments, so I'd rather trust the sat nav if you don't mind.' If you really want to, it can be helpful to learn some markers to help drivers find your house, especially in the dark. 'Just before the second set of lights' is imprinted on my brain for this reason.

Something technology will never replace is drivers moaning at you about roadworks and traffic, or asking you unanswerable questions about cars. This is usually forgivable, depending on how they react when you can't respond in the way they'd like.

A neurodivergent's guide to driving: My long and winding road to passing a driving test

Four years before I knew I was dyspraxic and decades before ADHD had even crossed my mind, my first attempt at learning to drive was *the* biggest inkling I'd ever had that I might not be able to do things other people take for granted at a certain age. My favourite person at the time, who was a decade older than me, told me flippantly that she'd passed her test just weeks after turning 17 and I was determined to do the same. The day after my 17th birthday, I booked six lessons over the phone with one of the big driving schools and keenly took to the road. My keenness didn't last long. By the third lesson I could hardly get the car out of first gear. The driving school had a funky illustrated progress booklet where you got graded from 1 to 5 for different skills and I was still at 2 'With difficulty'.

My driving instructor seemed baffled by my lack of progress. He tried to reassure me, but then warned me that if I didn't get better, we'd have to have 'some pretty serious talks'. He asked if there was anything in my life so far that suggested I might struggle with driving. I couldn't think of anything, probably because there were too many possibilities to narrow it down. Unlike many of my friends' parents, mine wouldn't pay towards lessons or a car, which led to many rows at home because it felt cruel of them to deny me something so vital to my future independence. The unspoken part was that they didn't want to spend a lot of money on yet another thing I'd give up when it felt too hard, or I got too scared. I couldn't afford to pay to learn myself because the jobs I could do were the jobs you needed a car to get to.

A year later, I tried again with another instructor. This time, I aced clutch control immediately and was in fifth gear by the end of the first lesson. But everything that came after that was harder, my lack of an intuitive grasp of anything irritated him, and when I left for university, I don't think he was sad. I carried on learning briefly in my university town. My instructor there told me five minutes into our first lesson that I was clearly ready for my test, then told me after I'd booked one that my driving was bordering on dangerous and I should cancel my test or risk having it abandoned. Then, he tried to tickle me as I drove down a dual carriageway.

I tried again in my mid-twenties, but working and commuting long hours made me dangerously tired during my little spare time at the weekend, and having an instructor who was barely out of his teens didn't help. A couple of years later, I wrote an article for a national newspaper about dyspraxia and driving, interviewing learners and instructors about their experiences. After that, life got less and less conducive to learning, and I had to explain to people who sent me invites to car shows and asked me to give inspirational talks about overcoming disability that I had, in fact, pretty much given up on the idea and resigned myself to being the only person over 20 and under 70 on my local bus.

The year I ran a marathon in my early thirties, I decided I wanted to take on an even bigger challenge and finally pass a driving test. I struck gold and found a local instructor who specialized in neurodivergent learners. He was dyslexic, and in a typically neurodivergent way knew his job inside out and took everything he did extremely seriously. Best of all, he understood what I needed. Two years and four tests later, I finally heard the words 'You've passed', and wept as if I'd been reunited with a relative and got married on the same day.

Here's everything I've learned about being a learner, and my answers to common questions learner drivers have.

'What makes it harder to learn to drive if you're neurodivergent?'

Every neurodivergent person is different and not everyone will relate to all these, or relate to them to the same extent, but these are some reasons and ways you might find driving hard, especially if you're dyspraxic and/or an ADHDer.

- **Difficulty with hand-eye-foot coordination:** This can affect clutch control, steering or your ability to get to grips with car controls.
- **Difficulty telling left from right**, making it difficult to follow directions.
- **Difficulty with short-term memory**, making it harder to remember instructions or directions.
- **Difficulty judging speed and distance:** This is the most common reason I hear from dyspraxics who choose not to drive.

- **Difficulty with spatial awareness**, especially when parking or turning, so you might hit kerbs more often, or find parking confusing in general!
- **Difficulty managing attention**, so you find it difficult to prioritize what to look at.
- **Difficulty processing information from lots of different senses at once:** It might be difficult to listen to the radio or hold a conversation while you're driving.
- **Difficulty managing emotions**, especially fixating on mistakes (yours, other drivers' or both).

It's a pretty daunting and discouraging list, especially if you've never learned before. But don't despair! There's more in a moment about what can help.

'When should I learn to drive and how long will it take? Or should I ever?'

For those of us to whom it doesn't come naturally, deciding when or whether to learn to drive can be as hard as driving itself. In one sense, people who aren't allowed to drive at all, or who actively choose not to, have it easier as they can just do everything possible to accept it and organize their lives around it so that they don't miss out on anything because of it. People who can and want to learn to drive but find it much harder are still expected to treat driving as something they can just pick up and breeze through one day whenever they fancy it. For many neurodivergent people, it's about reaching a point where the benefits outweigh the literal and emotional cost. Even so, it's best to assume that it'll take you at least a year to learn, and not take a job or make any decision that depends on passing quickly. A big advantage of taking your time to learn to drive is that you learn to drive in different seasons and weather conditions.

Some statistics say that driving is harder as you get older. For me and every neurodivergent person I've ever spoken to, the opposite is true. Driving is pretty much the most executive-functioning-dependent activity there is and your executive function, however bad you think it is, has almost certainly got better since you were 17. The main advantage of learning when you're young and not working full time is having more time for lessons and giving yourself more choice of where to work at an earlier age.

'Do I have to tell anyone official in order to drive?'

If you're dyspraxic, autistic or have ADHD, then generally no, unless:

- Your job, or one you're applying for, involves driving for a living. Commercial driving jobs, like delivery driving, taxi driving or driving large vehicles, have strict medical checks that exclude many people from doing them, including people who wouldn't consider themselves to be disabled. You'll also almost certainly need to tell your employer about any medication you're taking. If you've been doing a driving job safely for years, finding out you are neurodivergent shouldn't change anything. If you've never driven commercially before, it's probably not the first career I'd recommend.
- You have certain co-occurring health conditions.

In the UK, the law says you have to tell the Driver and Vehicle Licensing Agency about any medical condition that affects your ability to drive safely, including epilepsy and seizures and some mental health, heart and eye conditions. If you're dyspraxic, autistic or have ADHD with no co-occurring conditions, finding an instructor willing to teach you to drive and passing your test are essentially taken as enough evidence that you're a safe driver, unless your health changes.

Every few years, there seems to be an internet rumour about changes to driving laws which could affect neurodivergent people, from 'More people are going to be made to declare certain conditions in order to be allowed to drive' to 'More people are going to made to retake their driving tests' or 'People are going to be stopped from retaking their driving test after a certain number of attempts'. But there's never really been any reason to think any of these things are ever likely to happen.

'What will help me learn to drive as a neurodivergent person?'

Here are some practical and emotional tips for getting behind the wheel.

Think of how you'll pay for a car before you learn to drive

Driving a used car that's old enough to vote and held together with sticky tape used to be a rite of passage. These days, people tend to lease newer cars, which works a bit like buying a new phone on contract, only, a couple of hundred pounds a month as opposed to 30 or 40. Driving a new car isn't a question of being flash, it's about safety. As with phones and other gadgets, some dyspraxics get so used to a particular make and model of car they never want to drive anything different and will just upgrade to newer versions of the same model every few years. One dyspraxic woman I know of has done this for 20 years.

Try to learn in the area you'll mainly be driving in

This will make a big difference to your confidence, unless it's a choice between driving somewhere local and driving with a better instructor, in which case choose the better instructor.

Try to book your lessons at the time of day you learn best, and stick to the same time
Realistically, you probably won't be able to clear whole days for driving lessons, but try not to fit too much into a day when you have your lesson, and expect that you'll feel nervous beforehand and tired afterwards. And as with all appointments, if you book at a consistent day and time, you'll be more likely to remember it!

Use any in-car technology that helps you
Most cars have certain features as standard, like parking sensors and a built-in sat nav. Some will also have things like lane assist and an assisted handbrake. Generally, the more assistive technology you have, the easier driving will be. Anything that bleeps, lights up or shows a message to you as a reminder will help you – as long as you know what it's for! Your instructor should talk you through all your learner car's features and how to use them well before your test, and go over them regularly to refresh your memory. If you're lucky enough to have your own car, ask if your instructor will teach you in it. This can make driving much easier for you later...

Once you're used to lessons, or have passed your test, try and book a motorway lesson
For many years, learner drivers weren't allowed on the motorway, but this has now changed. Although motorway driving may seem scary, neurodivergent drivers sometimes find them more comfortable places to drive as they're more predictable than other roads.

Drive an automatic (or switch to an automatic after you pass)
Automatic cars have been standard in North America for decades and are often recommended for dyspraxics who struggle

with clutch control. The only disadvantage of this is that you won't be allowed to drive a manual car later if you pass your test in an automatic, and because manual cars are still common here, most UK dyspraxics prefer to pass in a manual and switch to automatic.

Don't assume you'll necessarily always struggle with clutch control because you're dyspraxic. As with a lot of physical skills, even though it won't come naturally to you at first, once it's in your muscle memory and you're used to the car, you might be brilliant at it, as was the case for me. The examiner I passed with even quirked an eyebrow and congratulated me on the speed of my gear changes! But even if your clutch control is ace, you might find driving an automatic easier after you pass, because it reduces the number of things you have to do and remember at once.

There are different opinions about whether automatic cars are helpful for ADHD. Some ADHDers say they are because, as above, they lighten the load on the brain. Others say the need for gear changes helps with concentration.

Take breaks after manoeuvres and break down steps in whatever way works for you

When I was first learning with my neurodivergent-specialist instructor, he gave me a five-minute break after each manoeuvre to help my brain re-adjust to driving forwards. Although manoeuvres are hard even for neurotypical people, neurodivergent people can be better at learning them because we're used to breaking down and practising sequences. Notes in your phone, apps or old-fashioned cue cards are good for this.

Use coloured stickers as reminders

Coloured dots or stickers you can buy from anywhere that sells stationery are good ways of remembering left from right, reminding you where to focus, and where important features are around the car and under the bonnet.

Don't read internet message boards

All internet message boards can attract trolls, but nothing brings them out like a thread by an unconfident driver. Some of the nasties are probably acting out trauma from accidents, some are just nasty. Either way, you don't need to remind yourself that you share a motorway with them.

But do watch videos and use interactive maps

As someone who first learned to drive before social media, I was thrilled to find that some driving instructors post videos about driving and tutorials on YouTube. Google Earth and similar tools are good for looking up test routes and road layouts.

Get to know what affects your driving

Obviously, driving drunk or hungover is a no-no. But some common over-the-counter medications can affect driving and it's easy to forget to check the label. ADHD medication should make you a better driver, but in rare cases it can make you feel drowsy at first, so watch out for this if you're new to it. A big consideration for women, me included, is how your hormonal cycle affects your dyspraxia and ADHD symptoms, and whether this affects your driving.

'How do I find a good driving instructor?'

By knowing you have dyspraxia and ADHD, you're already infinitely increasing your chances of finding an instructor you can work well with. Like the one I passed with, an increasing number of instructors specialize in teaching neurodivergent or disabled learners. They might be prepared to travel further than other instructors to teach, and if you can find one at all local to you,

I'd heartily recommend going for them. If an instructor is neurodivergent themselves, you'll probably know the answers to many of these questions below before you have to ask. If they aren't, it's all the more helpful to find out.

How experienced are they and how well do they know the area?

I'm sure there are 21-year-olds who are more confident drivers than me and who can teach well. I don't believe there are 21-year-olds who can teach someone neurodivergent.

What made them want to become an instructor?

Neurodivergent people tend to do well with people who genuinely enjoy the job rather than people who didn't know what else to do. I know it sounds a bit like a job interview question, but if you make it sound casual and interested rather than bossy, they should be happy to answer.

Have they taught pupils who are neurodivergent, disabled or of different abilities? Do they understand and accept that driving isn't easy for everyone?

There's a very big difference between being able to do something well and being able to teach it. The first rule of being a good teacher is to understand that things don't come as naturally to everyone as they do to you. Neurodivergent people are often good teachers because we understand this. Beware of an instructor who guarantees you will pass after a certain number of hours, or only cares about how quickly they can get you to pass the test. If your instructor thinks driving is a matter of common sense, that is a big red flag. Driving is no more 'common sense' if you're dyspraxic or have ADHD than hearing is if you're deaf in one ear, and an instructor needs to understand that you'll benefit from support which other learners might not need as much.

Do they talk too much at the wrong time?
When you're learning early on, you need to be able to concentrate. If they yammer on about everything from their divorce to their views on traffic legislation, feel free to ask them nicely to not talk, and walk away if they still do.

Where will you be going and what will you be doing on your first lesson?
My first instructor told me I shouldn't 'still' only be on side roads or still need picking up from my house after three lessons. The instructor I passed with 15 years later took me out on side roads for two to three months before I went anywhere else. I've heard some terrifying first-lesson stories of people being sent out to huge city roundabouts. To avoid being thrown in at the deep end, ask your instructor to talk you through what a typical first lesson looks like before you commit to anything.

Will they let you cancel and re-book at short notice if anything affects your driving?
My best instructor's mantra was that being in the right headspace for lessons was more important than anything. I once cancelled a lesson because there was a puddle of milk on my kitchen floor and I had no recollection of how it got there, which didn't seem like a great frame of mind to jump in a car with. Of course, cancelling at short notice isn't generally a nice thing to do, but when it comes to your safety, forget 'nice'.

Will they keep their hands to themselves?
Sadly, there's usually only one way to find out if the answer is no. If you find yourself in that terrible situation, do what I should have done and report them.

As with any type of professional relationship, it's best to book just one lesson or session with an instructor first to see if you're a good fit for each other. If they offer big discounts for block bookings, you can always do this afterwards once you know you want to carry on.

'What can help me during my driving test?'

As you probably know, the UK driving test consists of a theory and hazard perception test and a practical test, and you have to pass the theory and hazard perception part before you take the practical. The thing to watch out for in your hazard perception test if you're dyspraxic is not to click the screen too often or too vigorously as the software can think you're trying to 'cheat'. If this happens, talk to your instructor and the test centre about ways they might be able to help you. If you haven't passed your practical test within two years of taking your theory test, you'll have to take it again (and pay again), so don't rush it!

When you book your practical test, the form will ask you to write down if you need any 'reasonable adjustments'. You can ask for instructions to be repeated, ask your instructor to give hand signals for left and right, or ask for instructions to be worded in the way you're used to. Examiners often switch off certain assistive tech such as parking sensors, and you may be able to ask for these to be kept on. The practical test has changed in recent years to include sat nav driving, which I found much easier than following directions. You don't need to specify your disability to do this, but it might help if you do.

If you struggle to get to sleep the night before your test, taking a herbal-based, over-the-counter sleeping tablet might be helpful. But book your test nearer the afternoon to make sure it's worn off in time. If you take ADHD medication, take it as normal before your test and try to book your test for when it kicks in.

No matter how rested and ready you are for your test, expect to feel nervous. Sitting a driving test with dyspraxia and ADHD, especially if you're unmedicated, which I was when I took mine, is possibly one of the hardest things you'll ever put yourself through in your life. It amounts to an hour of being watched and judged on everything in the world you find hardest, with a lot of uncertainty thrown in. My very neurotypical German cousin was so nervous during her tests that my uncle eventually asked a local driving examiner to sit with them in the family car and watch her drive without revealing who he was! Sadly, not living in a tight-knit German village, this wasn't an option for me, and I had to take my place in the test centre waiting room alongside several nervous teenagers and their boyfriends. Fortunately, I had the next best thing: a neurodivergent driving instructor who talked me through everything to expect on the day. Although the test is the same, all test centres will have quirks, so ask your instructor to do this for you too. Many test fails happen at test centres that tend to be in strange locations like industrial estates, so get your instructor to talk to you about anything to watch out for (but don't be too hard on yourself if you forget and fail...).

In a driving test, you're allowed up to 15 minor faults. My instructor told me that neurotypical drivers fail by racking up minors, whereas neurodivergent drivers do an otherwise perfect drive and fail on something major because of nerves. Exactly as predicted, I failed my first test with two minors, and one major for whacking into a kerb. Both the examiner and I came back several shades paler...

There are lots of urban myths around about driving tests and examiners, but it is true that examiners are human, and, like all humans, some are more helpful than others. The examiner I passed with on my fourth test had taken me for my second, which I only narrowly failed. We remembered each other and had got along well. I think this familiarity helped me relax.

'What happens after I pass?'

Look up 'How to learn to drive' online and you'll be scrolling all day. Look up 'What happens after you pass your test?' and you might not be. Driving opens up another world of things you've never thought about.

Cost

You probably don't need me to tell you that buying and running a car is expensive. A number of UK surveys suggest the average age people learn to drive has risen from 17 to 26 because of this. You can save a lot on petrol and road tax in the long run by buying an electric car, but the upfront cost is usually higher.

Getting used to a different car from the one you learned in

The first time you go out in a different car, old or new, it's a good idea to go to a car park and get used to the controls and how the car responds to you. The controls you'll need to get used to first are the seats, gears, lights, indicators and windscreen wipers. Don't be like me and forget to adjust the seats, with a panicking passenger beside you.

Finding places to park

Finding a space in an empty local car park is very different from finding a space in an unfamiliar car park with someone behind you. Apps like *Parkopedia* can help.

Getting petrol or charging your car

Getting petrol is one of those things that's easy for people who've always done it, but it might take you a few more goes before it becomes automatic to you. To avoid that sudden 'OMG, I've never done this before and I don't know how!' feeling, get your instructor to show you how it's done.

Looking after your car
You should keep some basic safety equipment (things like a warning triangle, torch and first aid kit) in your car, and in some countries, you're required to by law.

If you drink alcohol, remember when you can't drink
Having a car to go and see people is fun until you remember you can't drink with them once you're there. And I was a 38-year-old woman when I got my licence, not a teenage boy racer.

Having the right shoes with you
I know of a high-flyer who caused thousands of pounds' worth of damage to someone's house by ploughing into a wall while wearing the wrong shoes. Even flat shoes with thick soles can make clutch control more difficult. Keep a spare pair of driving shoes somewhere safe in your car for the times you forget.

Remembering to change your shoes, take everything out of your car and lock your car
I similarly once met a high-flyer who'd forgotten to change her shoes when she got out of her car and did a speech in her driving trainers until an assistant came huffing and puffing onto the stage carrying her work shoes in a plastic bag. It's easy to accidentally leave things in your car when all your attention has been on driving, especially if you're a new driver. Some cars will now prompt you to check for your phone or belongings when you switch off the engine. If you don't have a modern car, a personal assistant or other passengers to remind you, coming up with some memorable wordplay can also help. For instance, I realized a while ago that 'Where is my phone?' and 'Where is my bag?' fit the tune of the song 'Where Is My Mind?' by the Pixies. This continually amuses me and helps me keep track of my belongings when getting around.

Knowing when it's better for you not to drive

Things that affect your driving when you learn (like your sleep, hormones, mood and medication) will affect you after you pass. If you know certain things affect your driving, try to plan your driving around them, or think of alternatives to driving you can use as last resorts if you have to. You could use an app to help you set aside a pound a week towards an emergency travel fund, so that you can take a taxi or public transport instead if you need to.

Final thoughts

There are plenty of neurodivergent drivers and plenty of neurodivergent non-drivers. There are also those of us who don't fit neatly into either category.

Research in 2016 (Hull, 2016) found that around a million people with UK driving licences have rarely or never driven since passing their test, so you're in good company. And by the way, that one million includes me. Despite my brilliant instructor and my determination to pass, I struggled to adjust to driving an older, stereotypical lady car and lost my confidence; then the Covid-19 lockdown happened, and since then, I've moved to a new area. In many ways, having a licence but not using it can be more of a downer than never having passed. I'm hoping to take some refresher lessons once this book is finished, with the help of a more neurodivergent-friendly car.

The next chapter is about something that can also be messy, joyful or both: relationships.

CHAPTER 10: A QUICK RECAP

- Driving isn't something that 'just happens' for most neurodivergent people: it's possible, but it's a commitment.
- It's best to find a really good instructor, not just someone who can drive. There are driving instructors who specialize in teaching neurodivergent learners.
- There are lots of practical things to think about after you pass, which it's better to think about before you learn.
- It's okay if you don't want to drive, now or ever. Many of us learn later in life and some won't learn at all.

CHAPTER 11

Making Sense of Relationships

Or 'Why is There So Much Drama in My Life?'

This chapter is about relationships of all kinds and how neurodivergence can explain them. It's the most personal chapter I've written because, well, relationships are pretty personal – especially when they involve drama.

I will happily stand on a stage and tell people I once got confused by revolving doors and thought 1500 and 1,500 were different numbers. I'm less likely to stand on a stage and tell an audience that bringing home my first ever payslip led to a screaming family row which went on for hours, because I couldn't remember my exact salary or tax code when they asked, and they found it unbelievable that I'd forgotten such important pieces of information which were written on a piece of paper I'd had with me all day. Or, equally, how much I scared the first man I ever asked out with my long-term memory. I was talking to him about someone else who was important to me at the time, going over meetings we'd had over several years and referring to each one by date. He told me in no uncertain terms that having such a good memory for this sort of detail wasn't normal or acceptable to him. For years, I believed this too, and was careful not to let my good memory show in situations where it might be held against me and taken as a sign I was unhinged.

The first draft of a book I ever completed, after a great many abandoned attempts, won an Arts Council new writing bursary, which gave me access to a mentor. It was a chaotic memoir, poured out in a few months, which told the story in detail of my life from 18 to 30, including attempts to become an arts journalist, my dyspraxia diagnosis and the multiple bereavements during my twenties which led to me giving up, and how I became an unlikely distance runner. Or at least, that's what I thought it was about. As my mentor pointed out, it was actually about a long pattern of obsessing over people linked to one another, to an extent I either couldn't work because of it, or tried to make it into my job.

Although, unlike many of my media contemporaries, I managed to avoid addictive substances during my twenties, the thing that felt like an all-consuming addiction to me was other people and relationships. When it came to people in my life, I always had a handful of 'best' friends, a lot of acquaintances I never really bothered to get to know, and then one or two people I was absolutely obsessed with getting to know. When I was diagnosed with ADHD alongside dyspraxia, with the help of therapy and medication, I began to piece together the reason for all this, and more.

There are three parts to this chapter. The first is about ways that neurodivergence can influence relationships. The second is about sex and neurodivergence, which equally includes having, wanting and not wanting sex. The final part is about what are often the most difficult bits in relationships, from conflict to grief and loss.

Ways neurodivergence can explain your relationships

At the beginning of this book, I mentioned experiences that are common to neurodivergence in general. Below are some which are more specific to relationships. Like everything else in this book, they're based on my experience, but I'm using 'you' rather than 'I' statements here because I hear them many, many times from neurodivergent people, often women, I speak to and hear from every day.

You have both a strong fear and a strong need to do things with or in front of others
Like most late-diagnosed dyspraxics I know, my lack of wanting to do things with other people as a child was simply put down to shyness. Once when my mum gave me a magazine quiz called something like 'How Shy Are You?' I scrunched it up and howled in protest, which probably should've been the first clue I wasn't as shy as I might've seemed. But I gave in and let myself believe it too, until I was unhappy enough to look for a better explanation. The belief I just didn't want or need to be around anyone wasn't only wrong, but damaging. Because, although my dyspraxia and Anglo-German self-effacement made me self-conscious, my dopamine-starved brain also craved and needed the stimulation that went with being seen and heard. Not just sporty or practical activities, which I mentioned back in the last chapter where I wrote about taking up running, but speaking in public too. I've been doing speaking engagements for a decade, and although I still struggle to organize my thoughts – and I sound drunk if I don't use notes – I feel better afterwards every time.

You get bored of people very easily, or fixate on them very intensely
Fixation and hyperfocus, which are usually seen as being linked

with hobbies and interests or tasks, can also be linked to a person in different ways. Person fixation can be about love, lust, non-sexual admiration, fascination or dislike. It can happen when you've upset somebody unintentionally (or think you have) and feel 'stuck' going over and over the situation. You might feel the urge to know or find out all about someone, for any reason, or no big reason. I remember hearing that the best spies are those who get so hooked on finding information for its own sake they forget why they're doing it. This might be why the security services sometimes look for neurodivergent people when they recruit. Social media has made it easy, more common and socially acceptable to fixate on a person, and this also gives you a lot of dopamine.

If you find yourself Googling certain people or checking out their social media feeds first or last thing in the day, this might explain why, especially if you take ADHD medication that wears off in the evenings. Before I'd ever heard of person fixation, I saw it either as something good and fun that didn't need to be managed, or something shameful and bad that I needed to stop doing but couldn't unless my fixation object was completely removed from my life, as if I was an addict giving up drink or drugs. There are situations where stopping contact with someone altogether is absolutely appropriate – whether you met them online last week or they're your twin sister (look up 'abusive relationships' if you're not sure). But in most of my fixation situations, just having a name for what I was experiencing, and better communication on both sides, would have helped me manage things without the need for this. As I've mentioned before, it's also common for *anybody* to feel fixated after someone dies, especially if the death was sudden, so neurodivergence can be hidden by grief until it gets harder and harder to manage both.

You have very fixated beliefs about relationships or who you're drawn to

Fixation can also mean having very fixated beliefs about

relationships, which can help keep you safe or limit you. For example, if someone asked you out as a joke when you were 15, you might believe people who are nice to you never mean it. Or if someone reacts badly to you talking about an experience, you might feel that no one will understand.

You feel very intensely drawn to people you want to be like, especially people older than you
This is great if the person is supportive of you in a healthy way, but more problematic if you see yourself as broken and in need of fixing.

You feel very strongly attached to people who are like you
If you don't meet people like you very often, it feels incredibly special when you do, especially if it feels like more of a coincidence than an effort. I once made friends with someone in a queue because I heard him faintly humming an old song I liked. I've also struck up innumerable conversations with random people on trains after overhearing them talk about something important to me, whether it's dyspraxia, music or food.

Where this kind of an affinity can become a problem is when a shared interest or history feels so powerful and important to you that nothing else seems to matter. It's great that I'm with a man who shares my love of chocolate and pasta, but not so great that I wouldn't care if he was horrible to me, or married to someone else with six kids and living on the other side of the world…

You've felt preoccupied with how to label your feelings or relationships
Whether it's your taste in music or films, or something bigger, like your faith, politics, sexuality or gender, how, or whether, you choose to label yourself is up to you, and labels, like relationships, can change or stay with us as we go through life.

There are a few reasons why labelling might be especially important to you as a neurodivergent person. It could be because growing up neurodivergent, especially without support, means that you're very in touch with your thoughts and feelings, aware of ways you're different, and keen to find a community where you belong. It could also be because you tend to have intense, fast-moving emotions or be very analytical and precise with your words. If you're thinking 'Yes to both!' you've probably felt pretty confused at times in your life! None of these things, by the way, mean your feelings don't matter, or you shouldn't have the right to make decisions about your body.

There's some research which suggests a link between neurodivergence and LGBTQIA+ identities, specifically autism (Hartman et al., 2023), and although this doesn't explain how or why they're linked, again, it's an interesting intersection that lots of people experience. No one knows for sure what makes someone LGBTQIA+ and there probably isn't a single biological or genetic explanation.

Lots of micro-labels for sexuality and gender have become mainstream over the last decade or so. These new labels don't mean that the experiences themselves are new or unusual. There are people I know who wouldn't necessarily use a label, like, for example, asexual or greysexual,[1] but can relate to the experience. It's also increasingly understood that there are different sorts of attraction, and that fixation, which many neurodivergent people experience, can be non-romantic. This wasn't well understood when I was growing up, which meant I had trouble working out what some of my feelings towards others meant. From speaking to others, this seems to have been a common experience for neurodivergent women my age and over.

---

1   Greysexual or grey ace: someone who rarely experiences sexual attraction to other people, www.asexuality.org/?q=grayarea

You don't need to have had sex or been in a relationship to be sure of your sexuality, or prove it to anyone else. You can also be sexually or romantically experienced and unsure. But if you're unsure and inexperienced, spending time with similar-age, supportive people, if and where possible, might help clarify things for you in a positive way. For anyone struggling to understand their feelings towards others, I'd highly recommend a book called *Hopelessly Aromantic* by Samantha Rendle (2023), which I read recently to support a friend's self-discovery. It's primarily a support book for aromantic[2] and asexual people, but it's a great explainer of what different sorts of attraction are too. You can also find details of LGBTQIA+ support organizations at the end of this book.

What, sadly, can delay understanding yourself is being preoccupied with someone who isn't available to you in any meaningful way (see below).

You feel very strongly drawn to people who are unreliable, unpredictable or far away

I was once told I had a gift for bringing all sorts of different people to my life. In some areas of my life, like my career as a journalist, this was an advantage. Unfortunately, the one thing the people I was drawn to from such a diverse range of backgrounds tended to have in common was being famously unreliable. An ADHD doctor explained to me what might be behind this.

Unpredictable attention gives you a massive dopamine boost, which makes it feel exciting and makes you feel good about yourself in a way regular attention doesn't. It can be why some ADHDers enjoy meeting lots of new people. It might also

---

[2] Aromantic or aro: someone who experiences little or no romantic attraction to other people, https://lgbtqia.wiki/wiki/Aromantic_Spectrum

be the reason you feel very attached to someone even though you have very little actual contact, or your relationship is hard to label. This is what's known as intermittent reward and it's the idea that gambling and social media platforms are built around.

Another reason for being attracted to busy, unreliable or far away people is that getting their attention can make you feel really good about yourself, but having to try hard can make you feel as if you're not good enough at the same time. This pattern in life often gets attributed to having abusive or unavailable parents or a similarly unstable upbringing, which may or may not apply to you. For neurodivergent people, it might also be because of our uneven abilities, which can make us feel driven and ambitious at times but unworthy at other times.

Of course, it's absolutely possible to get along really well with someone who's very busy, far away or leading a different life from yours. The key to this, though, is managing your expectations and both wanting the same thing. Pinning your hopes of friendship or romance on a very different or distant person when you're very lonely is more likely to lead to disappointment.

You feel very drawn to people with problems

Growing up neurodivergent without support can make you drawn to people with problems. This is understandable, often healthy, and a sign of being a good friend. I have spent many dedicated hours making playlists and buying comforting chocolate for heartbroken friends, and have received plenty in return. What's less healthy is feeling responsible for helping people with no insight into their problems and no one else to talk to; or if time blindness means your life gets taken over by trying to help someone.

Being drawn to people who've experienced a lot of problems can also make you more likely to experience complicated grief and loss. There's more on this at the end of the chapter.

You really value your friendships
To a greater or lesser extent, I think most neurodivergent people I've come across would say they find it hard to make and keep friends. For some, the communication differences that go with their neurodivergence have led to a lot of painful rejection all the way through life. Other neurodivergent people might fear rejection more strongly than they experience it. Either way, friendship is rarely something we take for granted, even as we get older and busier. Most of my close friends have been in my life for decades and most who didn't know earlier now recognize they're neurodivergent. Some of my friendships started because of specific difficult experiences we shared, which are now distant enough for me to have forgotten. I met my partner through my best friend when some of my friends had already had multiple marriages and children, and although a small part of me wishes we'd met sooner, I'm all the more grateful because we didn't.

Neurodivergence and your sex life (or 'Sex talk that doesn't sound as if it's from your embarrassed aunty'...)

You might not have realized that neurodivergence has an impact on your sex life, or you might have thought so but not known where to talk about it. In the introduction to this book, I mentioned the cringey paragraph on dyspraxia and sex I read when I was younger and promised you something better. Here it is...

What actually counts as sex?
To some people, this is a quick, simple question with a quick, simple answer. If you're neurodivergent, as with all questions, it's less likely to feel that way. In an intimate or a social situation, what counts as sex to you doesn't really matter as long as

everyone else involved consents to it and agrees with you. If not, your disagreement is the problem, not your definition.

In a medical situation, what counts as sex is anything you can get a sexually transmitted infection from doing, which includes things that people often think 'don't count'. If a doctor or health professional asks whether you're sexually active – or sexually active 'at the moment' – you should say yes if you've had skin-to-skin, genital contact with anyone of any gender and haven't had an STI test since. How long ago or how often doesn't matter. Otherwise, the simplest answers are no, not at the moment, or not since your last test.

Do neurodivergent people have less/more sex than other people? Why?

There is no 'right' amount of sex to have and nothing about a person inherently means anything about what they're like in bed. But there are ways the sex you're having or not having might be related to your neurodivergence.

Body image and attitudes to sex

Things we're told about our bodies can affect how we feel about sex, and this is especially true for neurodivergent people. Bodily insecurity can make us have less sex, or more sex to compensate. As a child, I had an accident on holiday involving the saddle of an exercise bike and had to wee in pain into a bucket of warm water for days, with my parents watching. As much as I later tried to laugh it off, entertaining friends with the story of how I'd lost my virginity to a bike, it made me feel somehow violated.

As a teenager, I endlessly heard sex compared to dancing, sport and cars: not exactly a recipe for sexual confidence for the girl removed from ballet classes, picked last in PE, and seemingly unlikely to ever pass a driving test. I also came of age at a time which was in many ways more grimly misogynistic than today.

Thankfully, during my twenties, I started to learn from sex writers and educators online who cared about making sex chat more positive and inclusive.

No one has a right to sex, and you don't have to have sex at all, ever, if you don't want to. But denying yourself the chance to enjoy it because you think it's for teenage gymnasts is a massive waste. Sexual pleasure is for everyone: even people who make breakfast in bed for their partner and then accidentally step backwards into a finished bowl of cereal, as I did with one gentleman…

Sensory issues
The multitude of things going on in your mind and body all at once can make sex thrilling or overwhelming. A dyspraxic writer I know summed this up neatly by saying: 'I have two attitudes to sex: Don't touch me or don't stop.' Particularly if you're dyspraxic, you might sometimes find it hard to take the initiative because you're afraid of physically hurting someone, or getting hurt.

There are two ways to overcome this. The first, as with everything I've talked about in this chapter, is to stick to doing what you're most comfortable with and enjoy doing, and unapologetically take your time doing it. Sex on TV or in porn lasts for two minutes because nobody wants to sit and watch a naked stranger gently stroke their partner's hand or kiss their neck for an hour. Real sex can last for as long as you like, and hyperfocusing on simple touch can be lovely. Or you can tell someone there's something you've always liked to try but are nervous about in case it's painful for either of you, in which case, a good partner will be understanding and patient. It shouldn't need to be said, but anyone who tries to deny your pain or force you into doing things you don't want to do does not deserve to be anywhere near you.

Motivation

Finding and having regular sex – even the most casual, impersonal sex you can think of – takes a certain amount of effort. As I've talked about in previous chapters, being neurodivergent can mean you lack consistent motivation in your life, even for things that are fun. This might include sex, meaning you have less of it. Alternatively, having lots of sex, or risky sex, can be a way of getting attention and approval you don't feel you get from school, home or work. You can relate to both of these feelings equally at different times in your life.

As a teenager at an all-girls school, I worked hard to get top grades in my strong subjects and accepted that sex and boys were for later. But when university and my first job didn't introduce me to the love of my life, and my academic achievements didn't turn out to be as useful as promised, risky sexual shenanigans started to seem like a way to have fun and boost my confidence. After multiple bereavements, I went back to not wanting to have sex at all for a long time, until eventually meeting a lovely man.

Getting bored quickly, OR fixated easily

Neurodivergent people tend to fall between extremes of easily bored or clinging to a 'type'. Depending on where you fall between these extremes, and what your 'type' is, this can lead to more or less sex.

Fear about being judged for our sexual history

One way that neurodivergent people can get very hurt is by being very honest about our experience or inexperience, thinking our honesty is helpful, then finding ourselves being judged. If we've been honest in the past and it hasn't gone well, we can end up feeling too worried about being judged to want to have sex at all.

Your sexual experience or inexperience is nothing to be ashamed of, but that doesn't mean you need to make it every partner's business. There are some specific sexual details that it's important to be honest with your partner about, like your sexual health and relationship status. But telling people the number of people you've slept with or exactly when you last had sex is rarely helpful. Any decent person who's interested in having sex with you should be more interested in what you're doing with them now than what you've done or haven't done with other people before.

Difficulty finding the right contraception
For women who have sex with men, finding contraception that's easy to use, easy to remember to take and free from side effects can be a challenge. It's worth talking to a sexual health clinic to find a method that suits you. Hormonal contraception can interact with medication, so talk to your prescriber if you're unsure. Condoms, as you may be aware, are not exactly the most dyspraxia-friendly invention. It doesn't matter how many times I see sex tips for women that recommend putting on a condom with your teeth while blindfolded or some other elaborately sexy way, I'm not going to try. Sometimes this is suggested as a way of making women feel more included in sex, or as a sexy solution for men who find it hard to stay hard while wearing one.

If these are an issue for you, you can still leave the putting on to your partner and just touch or say encouraging things to them while they do it. Similarly, keeping a stash of condoms at home shows you're being proactive and not relying on him to take the responsibility. I started carrying condoms in my bag after I realized that the potential consequences of unprotected sex outweighed the potential embarrassment of them falling out. As with period products, putting them in a pocket inside your bag that you don't use for anything else can minimize the cringe potential.

Medication
Certain medications for ADHD, anxiety, depression and other conditions may make you want to have less or more sex.

> See 'Neurodivergent body behaviours that don't go in cute memes....' in Chapter 9 for more on this.

The people around you
Culture, religion and other factors alongside neurodivergence can all affect our attitude to sex. If you're having sex with anyone other than yourself, the person you do it with will influence how you feel about it too. This might seem obvious, but the number one way I've found to enjoy sex and overcome any barriers to enjoying sex is to have it with someone you actually like. If difficulties with controlling your attention or movements profoundly affect your sex life despite being in a loving and committed relationship, you might want to look into sex therapy.

> The next section of this chapter tackles some more big relationship topics.

The tough stuff in relationships: From conflict to grief

Neurodivergence and conflict in relationships or 'Why you end up in horrific arguments (and what to do about it...)'
One moment you're asking about something tiny, the next you're screaming at each other so loudly people can hear you

up the street. If this describes any relationship or group you're involved in, it's quite likely that more than one person involved is neurodivergent. In my experience, there are some common types of arguments in families or close relationships:

- **The 'This is actually about something else' argument:** Very common in people who haven't worked through past problems.
- **The tone argument:** You can't control your tone or volume of your voice and so sound aggressive when you don't mean to be. Or the point matters so much but the way you make it feels as if it shouldn't matter.
- **The 'wrong time, person place' argument:** You react to things immediately and the people in front of you aren't necessarily the right people to understand.
- **The 'What do you mean you can't remember?' argument:** Where one person sees the other's bad memory, lack of attention to detail or not following instructions as manipulative. The worst example of this was an argument about my first payslip, which I mentioned at the start of this chapter.
- **The 'different planet' argument:** You have different ideas about how things should be done, usually because of neurological and/or other differences.
- **The 'But why...?!' argument:** One person suddenly 'changes the rules' in a way someone else doesn't understand. Like the Christmas when suddenly it was decided it wasn't okay for me, an adult, to use the downstairs loo before dinner. This is very common in ADHDers who feel things intensely and act on the spur of the moment.
- **The 'Everyone is hungry and tired' argument:** Any of the above, but with added tiredness and hunger in the mix. These are common if you're neurodivergent as you're more likely to forget to eat or struggle to recognize you're hungry.

Arguments are especially hard in a family or relationship where everyone involved is neurodivergent because everyone's intense reactions feed off each other's, and above all, it's less likely you'll have learned to de-escalate. De-escalation can sound like this:

- 'This isn't really about...'
- 'Sorry, I overreacted.'
- 'Let's do this later.'
- 'HALT (Hungry, Angry, Lonely, Tired).' This is an acronym addicts in recovery use to recognize when they might be tempted to relapse, but it's also very useful in general if you find it hard to see the connection between how you're feeling and why you might be feeling it. Quite simply, when something doesn't feel right in my body – physically, emotionally or both – I try to remember the last time I ate, drank, calmed down, slept or spoke to anyone else. If I can't remember or I know it was too long ago, I know this is likely to be the reason. For example, I felt grumpy at breakfast this morning because I was tired from being woken by the early sunrise, so I nicely asked everyone to be gentle with me until I felt more awake.
- 'My medication is wearing off. I need some space.' If, like me, you take medication for ADHD, you may find that your feelings and reactions are more manageable when the medication is more active in your body – and you feel more sensitive and reactive before it kicks in or as it starts to wear off.

Recognizing healthy relationships

There's an excellent resource called *An Autistic Guide to Healthy Relationships* (Pearson et al., 2024), which has been co-produced by a team of researchers at Durham

University and autistic adults with wide-ranging professional and lived experience. Although it's specific to autism and not ADHD or dyspraxia, many of the points the guide makes are relevant to all neurodivergent people.

One especially important point I really like is that people often talk about relationships as being either healthy or unhealthy, and this can be misleading. Often, relationships aren't simply either one or the other from beginning to end. A relationship can change from healthy to unhealthy, or from unhealthy to healthy and back again.

Here's an example: Two people with very different lives might enjoy getting to know each other and find their differences intriguing or fun at first. Then one or both might start fixating on their differences in a negative way. Then they might realize what's happening and try to resolve this. Big changes in life can also create differences which make a relationship stronger, or which threaten the relationship.

Neurodivergence and grief

I touched on some of my own experiences of grief and how they're related to neurodivergence earlier in this book. But, as this chapter is about relationships, and grief is an unavoidable part of relationships, I feel it belongs here too. Many classic grief reactions (fixation or denial, intense emotions, difficulty concentrating and other executive functions) are similar to traits associated with neurodivergence, so it might seem hard to know where one ends and the other begins. But the death of a loved one can ramp up these traits and make them harder to live with.

If you know or suspect that someone was neurodivergent, this might also feel relevant to you after their death. It might be because of a neurodivergent trait you or they had, or an interest that defined your or their life. Or it might be that you feel that a lack of awareness or support contributed to the person's death. Difficulties that are understood to be associated with unsupported neurodivergence, like accidents, addictions, eating disorders and poor mental health, are all linked to early deaths and an increased likelihood of being bereaved.

Being made to feel that you're reacting to something in the 'wrong' way because of your neurodivergence is hurtful in any situation, but especially when someone dies. Finding a space where you're able to feel and react however you want to can be really important. If other people are affected by the same loss, it's also a good idea to ask them if they find it helpful before you share your feelings in detail, or pass on information they might not have known.

You can find support for bereavement at the end of the book.

Final (nice) thought

I'll end this chapter on an uplifting note. The relationship-driven memoir I wrote a few years ago turned into two books: the one you're holding, and a novel where I explore some of the subjects in more detail than a single chapter of non-fiction will let me. The final thing I want to do here is quote something a good friend once said to me: 'The day I call and ask you if you have any news and you say "Nothing much" is a day I hope I never see.'

I can't think of a better way to sum up what can make relationships with a neurodivergent person in them great.

In the next and final chapter of this book, I'll sum up everything I've written in the book with ten of my biggest neurodivergent life lessons.

CHAPTER 11: A QUICK RECAP

- There are ways neurodivergence can explain or affect your relationships with others, from who you're drawn to, to how you feel and identify. This can make life both interesting and exhausting.
- Being neurodivergent might also have an impact on your sex life in different ways. Again, this can make sex more or less enjoyable in different ways.
- Relationships are as much about the other person as they are about you. Being neurodivergent doesn't make you to blame for everything that goes wrong in a relationship. Relationships can also change as we go through life, without it being anyone's fault.

CHAPTER 12

Ten Things I Wish I'd Known in My Twenties

Or 'The Whole Book, Summed Up'

If you asked me how many books I read in a year I could probably tell you, or point you to a list on my phone which may or may not be up to date. If you asked me how many 'ten things' articles I read in a year, I couldn't even begin to tell you. To finish this book – or if you haven't got around to reading the rest – here's a 'ten things' list, pulling together some of my most important lessons I've learned in life.

1. **One person is never the answer to everything in your life.** Especially if they don't want to be, or think they are. A great deal of unhappiness in my life has come from believing one person alone was the answer to making it better. Lots of people have felt this way about someone else at one time or another, but I believe that being neurodivergent and tending to fixate kept me stuck in that mindset for too long. The less I felt fixated on one person

at a time, the more, eventually, I was able to benefit from the variety of support I really needed.

Similarly, relationships of any kind shouldn't revolve around trying to prove you're good enough for the other person. Of course, not all relationships can be close, or equal. As a writer, I know that conflict and differences between people make good stories. But nobody's part in your life determines your worth.

2. **You are not your job.** If you're the type of neurodivergent person with a standout talent or interest which you've turned into a career, that career can very easily turn into your whole identity, especially if you've been pursuing it from a very young age. Equally, if you've never known what you're good at, find it hard to commit things, or have never felt you had a choice in where you work, you can easily be made to feel you're not worth anything until you've found some big calling.

In my early thirties, I slowly abandoned the career in journalism I'd been working towards all my adult life and took up distance running – the last thing in the world I'd ever have expected to enjoy. I often say other personal losses led to this change because it's partly true and an easy thing to say. But I was also tired of trying to be part of something that had never seemed to want me in it and that I didn't even know if I wanted to be part of anymore. Since then, a new generation of brilliant neurodivergent writers, performers, journalists and campaigners has emerged. If you're part of it, or you want to be, go you! You are brilliant and vitally important.

3. **The times you are okay are good times to figure out what works for you when you're not.** 'It's okay not to be

okay' is the Marmite of mental health advice. It's a love or hate thing (for non-UK readers: Marmite is a spread with a very distinctive taste). If you've got this far into a book, I hope you already know it's okay not to be okay. If you're anything like me (again, if you've read this far, you probably are), what's harder is being able to imagine yourself in one state when you're in the other. A big lesson is if that something keeps distracting me, I should use the time when I'm feeling okay to work it out. Sometimes it's good to leave something for a better time. Sometimes the best time is now and leaving it until you finish a long project will just make everything you do harder than it needs to be.

4. **The right medication can be life changing, and there's nothing wrong with it.** A lot of people who've only ever needed medication for something temporary, like a minor injury, assume this is how all medication works. Some people need medication for life, just as they need glasses for life. If medication works for you, there is no reason to feel bad about it or to stop taking it, and you should never, ever stop taking it without medical advice.

5. **Lots of people you love are probably neurodivergent too.** I said it right at the beginning of this book and I'm saying it again at the end. It doesn't mean you should be responsible for who they are or what they do. It doesn't mean you're the person who should tell them (my answer to that dilemma is in Chapter 4, if you missed it). But it can help you understand why they are the way they are, how that might affect you, and why you might get along.

6. **You're allowed to have mixed feelings.** We often describe

someone as being 'mixed up' as though mixed emotions are a bad thing. Because we tend to have more intense feelings than others or find it harder to make decisions than others, we may tend to believe mixed feelings are bad. Mixed feelings aren't bad. They're actually very healthy when it comes to a lot of decisions, because life is complicated...no matter what choice you end up making.

7. **Some things you can only know by living.** A way some people try to compensate for the challenges of neurodivergence, especially ADHD, is by trying to plan for every possible outcome. This means you can end up beating yourself up for not being able to prevent bad or difficult things happening to you. Just as people who've been through a bereavement or something similar will torture themselves thinking what they could have done differently if they'd known this or that, neurodivergent people can be the champions of the 'if only'. You can't prepare for everything in life – whether it's a train delay or a trauma.

8. **Change isn't linear.** This one came from bestselling author and mental health campaigner Bryony Gordon, via her therapist. I remind myself of it when there seem to be more snakes than ladders. Just as feelings can be mixed, change doesn't always happen and then stay that way.

9. **Writing is about focus first.** I said at the beginning that this isn't a book of career advice, and it isn't. But I'm a writer, and as you're reading this, there's a good chance you enjoy writing. Lots of creative writing tips are about finding time in your life to write, having the right idea, getting it across in the right way, and getting it in front of

the right person. All these are important. None of them, though, are as important as being able to focus on your writing once you do have time. You can have the best ever idea and all the time in the world, but if you can't, literally, stay still for long enough to write, no one will know about it. If you struggle to focus, whatever diagnosis you have or don't, try to address this before you try to address *anything* else.

10. **You don't just have to be an expert on yourself.** If you're a neurodivergent young person with a new or recent diagnosis, you have something very important that I didn't when I was younger. You have a far better understanding of how your brain works and why, which gives you far more space to think about and do other things in life. Growing up, I was curious about everything and had all sorts of interests. But through my teens, into my twenties and beyond, those interests faded as I spent ever more time just trying to work out what was going on inside me and fighting with my brain to make it do things. I lost the space to care about other people, or connect with them in ways other than through mutual, intangible sadness.

    Though it's a privilege to be able to write this book, there are lots of things I'd prefer to be an expert in than my own mind: world literature, Italian food, the history of the Middle East, climate change, computer programming... I might even have found more uses for my encyclopaedic knowledge of 1990s TV soaps and music eventually, if I'd had better self-awareness earlier on. You have the time and the free space in your head to become an expert in anything you want, if you're not already. As someone once said to me: take it, run with it and have fun with it...

Finally...

Over the next, final few pages, you'll find links to information and support for all issues mentioned in this book.

Further Reading

This is a list of other brilliant books and writing by neurodivergent women. The titles here cover dyspraxia, ADHD, autism, dyscalculia, dyslexia and being multiply neurodivergent. Many mention experiences that are commonly linked to neurodivergence, like sensory sensitivity, OCD, chronic pain, addiction, eating disorders and being misdiagnosed. They're also filled with hope, encouragement, warmth and humour.

Dyspraxia

- *Caged in Chaos: A Dyspraxic Guide to Breaking Free* by Vicky Biggs. Although aimed at a younger audience, this teenage memoir is still a must-read for anyone of any age who wants to understand dyspraxia. In the introduction to the updated version, Vicky, who is now an adult, also writes about what she's been up to since the book was first published in 2005.

- *Stumbling Through Space and Time: Living Life with Dyspraxia* by Rosemary Richings. An essential dyspraxic memoir about becoming an adult, covering body image, relationships, work, driving, travelling and living away from home through a dyspraxic lens.
- *Hidden*, a play by Nicola Werenowska. The story of a woman with unrecognized dyspraxia finding out who she is as she falls in love and becomes a mother. The play went on a national tour in 2017. If you missed it, you can buy the playscript online from a choice of outlets.

ADHD

- *A Feminist's Guide to ADHD: How Women Can Thrive and Find Focus in a World Built for Men* by Janina Maschke. A much-needed deep dive into why ADHD is under-recognized in women, how it harms us and what needs to change, from hormones and healthcare to work and relationships.
- *Better Late Than Never* by Emma Mahony. A memoir about recognizing ADHD in later life.
- *Scatter Brain – How I Got Off the ADHD Rollercoaster and Became the Owner of a Very Tidy Sock Draw* by Shappi Khorsandi. Comedian Shappi Khorsandi writes about her path to diagnosis.
- *Dirty Laundry: Why Adults with ADHD are So Ashamed and What We Can Do to Help* by Richard Pink and Roxanne Emery. A support guide written by the duo behind the popular social media account @ADHD_Love. If you've ever cried about lost socks or misbooked train tickets in front of a bemused partner, this one's for you.

- *It's Not a Bloody Trend* by Kat Brown. Kat is a journalist, and one of those people I've always felt as though I know well even though we only know each other very slightly. When she announced her ADHD diagnosis close to mine, that feeling made sense. She's written this excellent explainer of what ADHD is and isn't.

Autism

- *Letters to My Weird Sisters: On Autism and Feminism* by Joanne Limburg. Joanne's late-diagnosed autism made her determined to speak to seek out other outsiders. Here, she writes letters to four misunderstood women from history about feminism, disability rights, social isolation, parenting and more.
- *Strong Female Character* by Fern Brady and *Drama Queen* by Sara Gibbs. These two brilliantly witty and raw memoirs are by women who are both autistic and both comedians.
- *The Electricity of Every Living Thing* by Katherine May, a bestselling author who writes beautifully about travel and nature. This is the story of how a 600-mile walk down the English coast led to her realizing that she's autistic.

Dyscalculia

- *Dyscalculia: A Love Story of Epic Miscalculation* by Camonghne Felix. Breaking up with someone is hard enough, but have you ever been through a breakup that's forced you to confront a lifelong struggle with maths? Camonghne Felix has, and she's written this great book about it.

Dyslexia

- *Dyslexia and Me: How to Survive and Thrive if You're Neurodivergent* by Onyinye Udokporo. Although it's probably the best-known type of neurodivergence, dyslexia is still misunderstood and stereotyped. This memoir is one that will change that.

Being multiply neurodivergent

- *How Not to Fit In: An Unapologetic Guide to Navigating Autism and ADHD* by Jess Joy and Charlotte Mia. Written by the founders of @IAmPayingAttention, the online community for autistic and ADHD women.
- *Girl Unmasked* by Emily Katy. A memoir about autism and ADHD.
- *Knowing No Boundaries: A Memoir of My Life with Dyslexia, Dyspraxia and Sensory Processing Disorder* by Hannah Daly. There are many books about dyslexia, fewer about dyspraxia and even fewer about the experience of both. Here's one.
- *That's the Way I Think: Dyslexia, Dyspraxia, ADHD and Dyscalculia Explained* by Dr David Grant. I spoke with Dr Grant at one of my first ever events on dyspraxia. This is his book of anecdotes and insights drawn from his long career as a psychologist in higher education.

Further Information and Support

These are some organizations that support people who are neurodivergent or provide support with other issues mentioned in this book.

Need help right now?

In the UK
- Campaign Against Living Miserably (CALM) www.thecalmzone.net
- Mind www.mind.org.uk
- Samaritans www.samaritans.org/how-we-can-help/contact-samaritan

In the US and worldwide
- Befrienders Worldwide https://befrienders.org
- Substance Abuse and Mental Health Services Administration (US) www.samhsa.gov

Types of neurodivergence

Dyspraxia
- Dyspraxia Magazine www.dyspraxiamagazine.com
- Dyspraxic Me https://dyspraxic.me.uk
- Dyspraxia/DCD Ireland www.dyspraxia.ie
- Dyspraxia Foundation USA https://dyspraxiausa.org
- DCD Australia https://dcdaustralia.org.au
- Dyspraxia Support Group of New Zealand https://dyspraxia.org.nz

ADHD
- ADHD Foundation UK www.adhdfoundation.org.uk
- ADHDadultUK www.adhdadult.uk
- ADHD Aware https://adhdaware.org.uk
- ADHD UK https://adhduk.co.uk/about-adhd
- CHADD (US) https://chadd.org

Autism
- Autistica www.autistica.org.uk
- Ambitious About Autism www.ambitiousaboutautism.org.uk
- Autistic Girls Network https://autisticgirlsnetwork.org
- Autistic Self Advocacy Network (US) https://autisticadvocacy.org

Dyscalculia
- Dyscalculia Association www.dyscalculiaassociation.uk
- National Numeracy UK www.nationalnumeracy.org.uk
- Dyscalculia.org (US) www.dyscalculia.org

Dyslexia
- British Dyslexia Association www.bdadyslexia.org.uk

- American Dyslexia Association www.american-dyslexia-association.org

Tourette's syndrome
- Tourettes Action www.tourettes-action.org.uk
- Tourette Association of America https://tourette.org

Support for all neurodivergences

- The Brain Charity www.thebraincharity.org.uk
- Different Brains (US) http://differentbrains.org
- Directory of Counsellors and Therapists Dealing with Neurodiversity (UK) www.counselling-directory.org.uk/service/neurodiversity.html
- Directory of Neurodivergent Therapists (Worldwide) https://ndtherapists.com
- Embracing Complexity https://embracingcomplexity.org.uk

Other support (A–Z)

Abuse
- NAPAC: For Victims of Childhood Abuse https://napac.org.uk
- Refuge https://refuge.org.uk
- SafeLives https://safelives.org.uk
- 24/7 Rape and Sexual Abuse Support https://247sexualabusesupport.org.uk or call 0808 500 2222
- National Domestic Violence Helpline (US) 1 800 799.SAFE (7233)
- RAINN: Rape and Incest National Network (US) https://rainn.org

Addiction
- Action on Addiction www.actiononaddiction.org.uk
- GamCare www.gamcare.org.uk
- Talk to Frank www.talktofrank.com

Anxiety
- Anxiety UK www.anxietyuk.org.uk
- Anxiety & Depression Association of America https://adaa.org

Bereavement
- Cruse Bereavement Care www.cruse.org.uk
- Sudden (for suddenly bereaved people) https://sudden.org
- Suicide&Co (support after suicide bereavement) www.suicideandco.org
- Understood: A Guide to Supporting Neurodivergent People Bereaved by Suicide https://hub.supportaftersuicide.org.uk/resource/neurodivergence-guide
- What's Your Grief (US) https://whatsyourgrief.com

Bipolar
- Bipolar UK www.bipolaruk.org
- Depression and Bipolar Support Alliance (US) www.dbsalliance.org

Chronic pain
- The British Pain Society www.britishpainsociety.org
- Pain Concern https://painconcern.org.uk
- US Pain Foundation https://uspainfoundation.org

Disability advice and campaign groups
- Benefits and Work (community-led support for disability and workplace benefits) www.benefitsandwork.co.uk

- Citizens Advice UK www.citizensadvice.org.uk
- Citizens Advice Australia https://cabwa.com.au
- Disability News Service www.disabilitynewsservice.com
- Disability Law Service https://dls.org.uk
- National Survivor User Network www.nsun.org.uk
- American Association of People with Disabilities www.aapd.com

Disabled living
- Essential Aids (accessible kitchen and home gadgets) www.essentialaids.com
- Simply Emma (accessible beauty products) www.simplyemma.co.uk

Eating disorders
- Beat www.beateatingdisorders.org.uk
- National Alliance for Eating Disorders (US) www.allianceforeatingdisorders.com

Epilepsy
- Epilepsy Action www.epilepsy.org.uk
- Epilepsy Foundation (US) www.epilepsy.com

LGBTQIA support
- Asexual Visibility & Education Network (AVEN) www.asexuality.org
- Biscuit (Support for Bisexual Women) https://thisisbiscuit.org.uk
- Galop (the LGBT+ anti-abuse charity) https://galop.org.uk
- Switchboard LGBTQIA https://switchboard.lgbt
- Stonewall www.stonewall.org.uk
- Trans Unite UK www.transunite.co.uk
- Outright International https://outrightinternational.org

OCD
- OCD Action UK https://ocdaction.org.uk
- International OCD Foundation https://iocdf.org

Sexual health and wellbeing
- Fumble https://fumble.org.uk
- Terrence Higgins Trust www.tht.org.uk/sexual-health
- American Sexual Health Association www.ashasexualhealth.org

Trauma
- PTSD UK www.ptsduk.org

References and Bibliography

Americans with Disabilities Act (1990) Accessed on 16/9/24 at: http://adata.org

Barnes, J. (2015) The Robert Peston Interview Show (with Eddie Mair). BBC Sounds. Accessed on 6/1/25 at: www.bbc.co.uk/sounds/play/b05xd69q

Biggs, V. (2014, first published in 2005) *Caged in Chaos: A Dyspraxic Guide to Breaking Free: Updated Edition.* London: Jessica Kingsley Publishers.

Brown, K. (2024) *It's Not a Bloody Trend: Understanding Life as an ADHD Adult.* London: Little, Brown Book Group.

CanChild (n.d.) Developmental Coordination Disorder. https://canchild.ca/en/diagnoses/developmental-coordination-disorder

Carder, M. (2024) *It All Makes Sense Now: Embrace Your ADHD Brain to Live a Creative and Colourful Life.* London: Hay House.

Children and Adults with Attention-Deficit/Hyperactivity Disorder (2018) Sunlight for ADHD: What the science says. Accessed on 16/9/24 at: https://chadd.org/adhd-weekly/sunlight-for-adhd-what-the-science-says

Daly, H. (2022) *Knowing No Boundaries: A Memoir of My Life with Dyslexia, Dyspraxia and Sensory Processing Disorder*. Ireland: Hannah Daly.

Donovan, D. (2022) *The Anti-Planner*. Nebraska: Slightly Salty Studios.

Flippin, R. (2024) Hyperfocus: The ADHD phenomenon of hyper fixation. ADDitude. Accessed on 16/9/24 at: www.additudemag.com/understanding-adhd-hyperfocus

Gillberg, C. (2024) Developmental Coordination Disorder. Gillberg Neuropsychiatry Centre at the University of Gothenburg. Accessed on 16/9/24 at: www.gu.se/en/gnc/developmental-coordination-disorder

Hartman, D. et al. (2023) *The Adult Autism Assessment Handbook: A Neurodiversity Affirmative Approach*. London: Jessica Kingsley Publishers.

Hewson, A. (2024) *Neurodiversity in the Workplace: How to Create an Inclusive and Safe Environment*. London: Trigger Publishing.

Hollander, J. (2022) Millions of Americans have my invisible disability. You've probably never heard of it. Accessed on 16/9/24 at: www.marieclaire.com/health-fitness/a35292137/dyspraxia-developmental-coordination-disorder-in-america

Hull, R. (2016) Almost a million UK licence holders haven't driven since passing their test – watch what happens when 'parked' motorists get back behind the wheel. This is Money. Accessed on 6/1/25 at: www.thisismoney.co.uk/money/cars/article-3837905/Almost-1m-UK-licence-holders-haven-t-driven-passing-test.html

Khorsandi, S. (2023) *Scatter Brain: How I Finally Got Off the ADHD Rollercoaster and Became the Owner of a Very Tidy Sock Drawer*. London: Ebury Publishing.

Mahony, E. (2021) *Better Late Than Never: Understand, Survive and Thrive; Midlife ADHD Diagnosis*. London: Trigger Publishing.

McCabe, J. (2024) *How to ADHD: An Insider's Guide to Working with Your Brain (Not Against It)*. Philadelphia: Rodale Books.

McNicoll, E. (2020) *A Kind of Spark*. London: Knights of Media.

Pearson, A. et al. (2024) *An Autistic Guide to Healthy Relationships*. Accessed on 16/9/24 at: www.durham.ac.uk/news-events/latest-news/2024/04/autistic-guide-to-healthy-relationships

Price, D. (2021) *Laziness Does Not Exist: A Defence of the Exhausted, Exploited, and Overworked*. New York: Atria Books.

Rendle, S. (2023) *Hopelessly Aromantic: An Affirmative Guide to Aromanticism*. London: Jessica Kingsley Publishers.

Richings, R. (2022) *Stumbling Through Space and Time: Living Life with Dyspraxia*. London: Jessica Kingsley Publishers.

Roper, M.F. (2020) Why I'd Rather Make a Wedding Cake for You than a Sandwich. Accessed on 16/9/24 at: https://maxinefrancesroper.medium.com/why-id-rather-make-a-wedding-cake-for-you-than-a-sandwich-ee459b4e55db

Science Daily (2013) Do sunny climates help ADHD? Accessed on 16/9/24 at: www.sciencedaily.com/releases/2013/10/131021094644.htm

Smale, H. (2023) *Geek Girl* (10th anniversary edition). London: Harper Collins. (Book 1 of a 6-book series. First published in 2013.)

Welding, J. (2023) Students with Disabilities in Higher Education: Facts and Statistics (US). Accessed on 16/9/24 at: www.bestcolleges.com/research/students-with-disabilities-higher-education-statistics/#disability-financial-aid-and-student-loan-forgiveness

Acknowledgements

Though writing a book is often seen as a solitary thing, there are usually many people who make it possible. This is especially true if you grow up in a world not designed for you. I'm very fortunate to have always had people in my life who, although we haven't always understood each other well, have ultimately wanted the best for me and supported me in lots of ways to do what I'm best at. Thank you to all my family, to Andy, my wonderfully patient partner, and to my loyal friends and colleagues for all your patience – and chocolate!

Thank you to Aggie Stewart for being the brilliant editor I've always needed, and to everyone at Jessica Kingsley Publishers who has supported this book. I am also grateful to The Society of Authors for a grant that helped me at an important stage of the writing.

Thanks to so many talented women for writing about their neurodivergence and/or mental health, including Nicola

Werenowska, Vicky Biggs, Rosemary Richings, Joanne Limburg, Alice Hewson, Rae Earl and Bryony Gordon.

Having been born very prematurely (I've never had a straightforward relationship with time...) I literally owe my life to more health professionals than I'll ever know. Special thanks to Paula Kelly and the late Dr Leon Gerlis.

This book largely exists because of Dr Stephen Humphries, who diagnosed my ADHD in 2020 and sadly died suddenly, shortly after I finished writing it.

Several more people who, in their own ways, taught me a lot about life sadly aren't here for me to thank, but will never be forgotten.

Finally, thanks to Allan Wilson, who supported me as a young writer on condition that I do something to help others one day. I hope I've honoured that here.

Index

A

accidents 198
addictions 181–3
ADHD
    causes of 42–3
    and DAMP (Disorders of Attention, Motor Skills and Perception) 41–2
    description of 32
    diagnosis of 58–83
    and dyspraxia 31
    and executive function 32–4
    fixations in 34–5
    further reading on 252–3
    hyperfocus in 34–5
    misconceptions about 37–40
    'strengths first' description 28
    types of 36–7
ADHD UK 154
Adult ADHD Self-Report Scale (ASRS) 70
alcohol 181–3
alert cards 97
'all or nothing' in neurodivergence 46
Americans with Disabilities Act (1990) 61, 64
anger after diagnosis 86–7
Anti-Planner, The (Donovan) 17
assessments for ADHD/dyspraxia 72–7
Australia
    diagnosis of ADHD/dyspraxia in 61
autism
    diagnosis of 76
    and dyspraxia 31
    further reading on 253
Autistic Guide to Healthy Relationships, An (Pearson) 241

B

Barnes, Julian 146
beauty tips 192–6
benefits claims
    and diagnosis of ADHD/dyspraxia in 60, 63
Better Late Than Never (Mahony) 27
Biggs, Vicky 23
birth experiences
    and neurodivergence 50–1
body-focused repetitive behaviours (BFRBs) 196–7

INDEX

body image 235–6
boredom
    and ADHD 39
    and sexual desire 237
brain damage
    and neurodivergence 41

C

Caged in Chaos (Biggs) 23
Canada
    diagnosis of ADHD/dyspraxia in 61
CanChild 61, 200
Carder, Meredith 17
Centers for Disease Control and Prevention (CDC) 61
Children and Adults with Attention-Deficit/Hyperactivity Disorder 200
Citizens Advice 198
coaching for neurodivergence 153–8
combined ADHD 37
compliments 110
conflict in relationships 239–42
confusion after diagnosis 86
Conners' Rating Scale for ADHD 75
contraception 238
counselling
    and neurodivergence 49–50
    as support 149–53
creative writing 248–9
criticism and neurodivergence 52–3

D

Daily Telegraph, The 24
DAMP (Disorders of Attention, Motor Skills and Perception) 41–2
diagnosis of ADHD/dyspraxia
    assessments for ADHD/dyspraxia 72–7
    benefits of formal diagnosis 59–64
    in different countries 60–2
    myths about 65–7
    places for 67–9
    referrals from GP 69–71
    self-diagnosis 79–81
Diagnostic and Statistical Manual of Mental Disorders, fifth edition (DSM-5) 75

difficult situations 52
Dinosaur (TV sitcom) 27
Disabled Students Allowance (DSA) 59
disclosure of neurodivergence
    after diagnosis 89–94
    at work 99–102
discrimination
    as reaction 115–19
    in work 116–17
DIVA (Diagnostic Interview for ADHD in Adults) 75
Donavan, Dani 17
doubts
    dealing with 55
driving
    author's experience of 209–11
    positives of not 203–9
    questions for learners 211–24
drug taking 181–3
dyscalculia 42, 253–4
dyslexia 30–1, 76, 254
dyspraxia
    as autism/ADHD lite 31
    causes of 42–3
    and DAMP (Disorders of Attention, Motor Skills and Perception) 41–2
    description of 19, 28–9
    diagnosis of 58–83
    and dyslexia 30–1
    further reading on 251–2
    misconceptions about 30–1
    'strengths first' description 28
    and typing 25–6
    as under-recognized condition 29–30
Dyspraxia Collective 126–7
Dyspraxia Foundation USA 61, 127

E

'easy' and 'hard' tasks with neurodivergence 48
emotional management
    and ADHD 33
Equality Act 63–4
executive dysfunction
    and ADHD 37–9
executive function 32–4
exercise 186–8

F

family traits of neurodivergence 51
fashion tips 192–6
fixations
   in ADHD 34–5
   and sexual desire 237
Flippin, R. 198
food 176–81
form-filling 98
friendships
   and neurodivergence 51
functioning labels 20

G

Geek Girl (Smale) 27
General Medical Council (GMC) 117
Gillberg, C. 200
GP referrals 69–71
grief 242–3
Guardian, The 24

H

happiness after diagnosis 85–6
Hartman, D. 231
healthcare
   discrimination in 117–18
healthy living
   and alcohol 181–3
   and drug taking 181–3
   and exercise 186–8
   and food 176–81
   and periods 188–90
   and sleep 183–6
   and smear tests 190–2
Hewson, Alice 17
holding back 54
Hollander, Jenny 61
Hopelessly Aromantic (Rendle) 232
hormones 50
How to ADHD (McCabe) 17
Hull, R. 224
hyperfocus
   in ADHD 34–5
   and medication 173

I

identity-first language 19–20
inner critic 140–9
intelligence tests 48
interoception 33
Ireland
   diagnosis of ADHD/dyspraxia in 60
It All Makes Sense Now (Carder) 17

J

justifying yourself 52

K

Khorsandi, Shappi 27
Kind of Spark, A (McNicoll) 10, 27
Kirby, Amanda 24

L

lanyards 97
laziness
   and ADHD 37–9
Laziness Does Not Exist (Price) 37
LGBTQIA+ identities 231–2
life after diagnosis
   alert cards and lanyards 97
   different feelings 85–7
   disclosure of neurodivergence 89–94
   learning more about neurodivergence 88–9
   suspicions about neurodivergence in others 94–6
life changes 54

M

Mahony, Emma 27
masking 46–7
McCabe, Jess 17
McNicoll, Elle 10, 27
media appearances 128–31
medication
   importance of 247
   as last resort 161–2
   myths about 165–9
   problems with 164–5

INDEX

and sexual desire 197, 239
and sleep 184-5
tips on using 169-73
workings of 162-4
meeting other neurodivergent people 88
memories after diagnosis 86
mental health issues
   coaching for 153-8
   and inner critic 140-9
   and neurodivergence 49-50
   okay/not okay 246-7
   support for 149-59
mixed emotions 249
monotropism 35
Murray, Dinah 35
myths about diagnosis of ADHD/dyspraxia 65-7

N

National Institute for Health and Care Excellence (NICE) 71
negativity
   and neurodivergence 40-1
neurodivergent
   description of 18-19
neurodiversity
   description of 18
   diagnosis of 81-2
   misconceptions about 40-2
   reactions to diagnosis 84-103
   and self-understanding 45-57
Neurodiversity in the Workplace: How to Create an Inclusive and Safe Environment (Hewson) 17
neurotypical
   description of 19
New Zealand
   diagnosis of ADHD/dyspraxia in 61

O

object permanence
   and ADHD 39
online sharing 126-8, 134-7

P

past relationships 119-23

Pearson, A. 241
peer support 158-9
perceptions of others 49
periods 188-90
person-first language 19-20
personal hygiene 197
Personal Independence Payment (PIP) 198
personality traits
   and neurodivergence 56-7
places for diagnosis of ADHD/dyspraxia 67-9
planning
   and ADHD 33
predominantly hyperactive and impulsive ADHD 36
predominantly inattentive ADHS 36
Price, Devon 37
prioritizing
   and ADHD 33
psychometric tests 49
public speaking 131-2

Q

quirkiness
   and neurodivergence 40

R

reactions of others
   bad reactions 112-14
   best reactions 105
   common questions 106-10
   common types of 105-6
   compliments 110
   discriminatory 115-19
   past relationships 119-23
   reacting to questions 110-11
   reading reactions 111-12
regrets after diagnosis 86-7
rejection and neurodivergence 52-3
relationships
   conflict in 239-42
   importance of 245-6
   neurodivergent experiences of 228-34
   past relationships 119-23
   and sexual desire 234-9

relief after diagnosis 85
Rendle, Samantha 232
Richings, Rosemary 10–11
ruminating after diagnosis 87

S

Scatter Brain (Khorsandi) 27
Science Daily 200
self-diagnosis 79–81
self-monitoring
    and ADHD 33
self-understanding of neurodiversity 45–57
sensory issues 236
sexual desire 197, 234–9
sharing experiences
    decision to 125–6
    media appearances 128–31
    online 126–8, 134–7
    payment for 133–4
    privacy issues 137–8
    public speaking 131–2
    in research 132–3
short-term memory 32
Singer, Judy 18
sleep 52, 183–6
Smale, Holly 27
smear tests 190–2
South East Asia
    diagnosis of ADHD/dyspraxia in 61–2
Storrie, Ashley 27
Stumbling Through Space and Time: Living Life with Dyspraxia (Richings) 10
'suffering' as description 20
support for mental health issues 149–59
suspicions about neurodivergence in others 94–6

T

teenage years
    difficulties of 53–4
'thinking' and 'doing' gap with neurodivergence 48
tidiness 198
Tumi (aka The Black Dyspraxic) 126
types of ADHD 36–7

U

United States
    diagnosis of ADHD/dyspraxia in 60–1

W

weather 199–201
Wechsler Adult Intelligence Scale (WAIS) 74
Welding, J. 59
'Why I'd Rather Make You a Wedding Cake for You than a Sandwich' (Roper) 177
women
    and diagnosis of ADHD/dyspraxia 73
    experience of neurodivergence 52
    and medication 164
    and periods 188–90
    and smear tests 190–2
work
    disclosure of neurodivergence 99–102
    discrimination in 116–17
    driving to 205–6
    importance of 246
    support for 63–4